Mommy, How Does God Speak to You?

Renee Allen

All Scripture quotations, unless otherwise indicated, are taken from the *Holy Bible, New International Version*®, **NIV**®. Copyright ©1973, 1978, 1984, 2011 by Biblica, Inc.™ Used by permission of Zondervan. All rights reserved worldwide. www.zondervan.com The "NIV" and "New International Version" are trademarks registered in the United States Patent and Trademark Office by Biblica, Inc.™

Scripture quotations marked **ESV** are taken from *The Holy Bible, English Standard Version*. ESV® Bible (The Holy Bible, English Standard Version®), copyright © 2001 by Crossway, a publishing ministry of Good News Publishers.

Scripture quotations marked **NKJV** are taken from the *New King James Version*®. Copyright © 1982 by Thomas Nelson. Used by permission. All rights reserved.

Scripture quotations marked **NASB** are taken from the *New American Standard Bible*®, Copyright © 1960, 1971, 1977, 1995, 2020 by The Lockman Foundation. All rights reserved.

Scripture quotations marked **NLT** are taken from the *Holy Bible, New Living Translation*, copyright © 1996, 2004, 2015 by Tyndale House Foundation. Used by permission of Tyndale House Publishers, Inc., Carol Stream, Illinois 60188. All rights reserved.

Copyright © 2023 by Renee Allen

All rights reserved. No part of this publication may be reproduced, stored in a retrieval system, or transmitted in any form or by any means. – electronic, mechanical, photocopy, recording, or any other-except for brief quotations in printed or digital reviews without the prior written permission of the publisher.
ISBN – 9798397966603

DEDICATION

For Mike, Lindsey and Anthony, Michael and Ashley

Thank you...

...For giving me the gift of your time, and for being vulnerable,
and yet strong enough, to allow me to write your stories.
...For always asking how the book was coming,
for holding me accountable to finish,
and for not allowing me to give up
when the mountain seemed too high.
...For the many God conversations we have,
that always leave me wiser,
and so very grateful for each one of you.
...And for believing in me, when I didn't believe in myself.

For Boone, Gracelyn, Liliana, Gavin
and the Yet to Be Born Precious Little Ones

Lord, thank you for these precious little ones whose lives You have vested into our care. Help them to come to love You deeply from a very young age and help us to teach them to recognize and know Your Voice.

To My Little Buddy Taz

...whom I said goodbye to during the final weeks of finishing this book. I miss you Tazer...I will always miss you.

...I miss having you sit by my side, on my lap or within my reach as I write. Your presence has always comforted me when I wept over a hard memory and calmed me as I struggled to find words for what I needed to say. You were, and always will be, my best buddy...and I will always love you.

Contents

Preface		1
Introduction: About This Book		5
Chapter 1	Teaching Your Children to Recognize and Know God's Voice	7
Chapter 2	God Speaks Through Answered Prayer	19
Chapter 3	God Speaks in a Still, Small Voice	33
Chapter 4	God Speaks Through His Word	47
Chapter 5	God Speaks Through Peace	63
Chapter 6	God Speaks Through Dreams	79
Chapter 7	God Speaks Through Unanswered Prayer	87
Chapter 8	God Speaks Through Our Thoughts	99
Chapter 9	God Speaks Through His Holy Spirit	107
Chapter 10	God Speaks Through Discernment	117
Chapter 11	God Speaks Through Circumstances	131
Chapter 12	God Speaks Through Prayer, Worship and Praise	145

Preface

The Journals

In 1989, when I became pregnant with my first child Michael, I began writing to him, and later to my daughter Lindsey, in separate journals. At that time, unbeknownst to them, I made a promise to them, and to God, that I'd do my best to document the things God did in our lives. I call these stories "God Stories".

God Stories are the stories of when I, or those in my family, witnessed God at work in our lives. Sometimes God worked in big and powerful ways, and sometimes He worked in small and intimate ways. The God Stories of our lives are stories of good times, as well as stories of the not so good times. They are stories of achievement, triumph and abundant blessing, as well as stories of failure, pain, hurt and questioning. The stories are filled with praise, joy, gratefulness and thankfulness, as well as struggles, challenges, waiting and doubt. God has written, and continues to write, many kinds of stories in our lives.

My prayers also fill the well-worn pages of each of my handwritten journals. From the first page to the last, there are all kinds of prayers. Prayers when I thanked God and prayers when I doubted God. Prayers only my heart heard and prayers when I cried out loud to God. Prayers I was too embarrassed to share with anyone but God and prayers when I was in awe of God. Prayers of thanksgiving and praise when God showed up in ways I never could have imagined, and prayers when I didn't know how or if God would show up…but hoping He would.

Some of the pages in the journals are stained with tears. For many reasons, those are the hardest pages to read. For those are the pages when God listened and held me in His arms, as my spirit shattered or my heart broke in two.

All of it is there…laid bare on the well-worn pages of the journals. The laughter, the pain, the joy and the praise. It's all there as a living testimony of my very big and wonderful God.

The God Stories in all those hand written journals are now the heartbeat of "Mommy, How Does God Speak to You?"

The Power of a Single Story

People have been telling stories since the beginning of time. Before people were able to write, use paper, tablets, computers or keyboards, they told stories. Through the telling of stories, history, knowledge, wisdom and insight were shared from one generation to the next. Throughout history, the survival of man often hinged on the knowledge that was passed down through a story. The power of a single story should not be overlooked.

Today, we listen to stories, first as children, and then throughout our lifetimes as adults. Stories are memorable and impactful and they often create an emotional connection. Stories inspire us and make us feel. And they empower us. Stories can cause us to act and make decisions, that ultimately can change the course of our lives.

People tend to remember the stories they hear because stories are easy to recall. Stories are often easier to remember than things we read in a text book, or things we see on the news or on the internet.

True stories are especially powerful. They reach into the heart and stir the soul. True stories are testimonies. And testimonies are the impactful stories God has written into our lives. And as we share our testimonies, God uses our stories to impact the lives of others.

Jesus often taught by telling stories. He modeled for us how we could use a story as a tool to teach and help others. If Jesus taught using stories, shouldn't we do the same?

Make Them Known to Your Sons and Grandsons

In Deuteronomy 4:9 God commands us not to forget what He has done. Not only are we to remember what God has done, but we are commanded to share and repeat what God has done, to our children and grandchildren.

But watch out! Be careful never to forget what you yourself have seen. Do not let these memories escape from your mind as long as you live! And be sure to pass them on to your children and grandchildren. - Deuteronomy 4:9 NLT

The New American Standard Bible gives us more to consider...*Only give heed to yourself and keep your soul diligently, so that you do not forget the things which your eyes have seen and they do not depart from your heart all the days of your life; but make them known to your sons and your grandsons.*
- Deuteronomy 4:9 NASB

Teaching our Children to Recognize and Know God's Voice

I never imagined God would call me to share my journal entries in a book. A book that would impress upon parents the profound responsibility we all have. The responsibility to teach our children to recognize and know God's voice and to tell God's Stories to our children.

I hope that God will use the stories in this book to guide, comfort and encourage my children and grandchildren as they walk through the valleys and mountains of life. In addition, my faith leads me to believe that perhaps God will also use these stories to impact the lives of others and help other parents and grandparents in their quest to teach their own children about God.

The stories in this book are from the 1970's to present day. They are true. They happened. Although I've taken creative liberties with some of the small details of each story, the stories themselves, and the parts regarding what God did, are true.

As you read through the chapters, I pray that God will create a stirring in your heart that will cause you to begin to document your own God Stories. I also pray you will begin to share your own God Stories, over and over and over again, with your own children and grandchildren.

Introduction
About This Book

This book is a collection of true stories. Each story was taken from memory or from one of several journals in which I documented true life events spanning across more than five decades.

The Recipe

This book was written using a God given recipe for each chapter. As a result, each chapter is divided into three sections, each with a specific purpose.

- ### The Year and/or Date

  This is the year in which the story took place. These dates are not made up. They are either referenced in the journals or research was completed to determine the exact year in which the story took place.

- ### The Story

  Each story is a true story about what God did in my life or in the lives of those in my family. Each story has been used at some point in the lives of my children, to help them not only recognize and know Gods voice, but to teach them about who God is and what His Word says.

- ### *A Mother's Thoughts*

  These are the personal thoughts I've felt led to share. I'm grateful for the freedom God gave me in this section. This is the section where I express myself, share my heart, share the back story of the story or share whatever else God brought to mind at the time of writing the story.

- Take Aways

Takeaways are the things we "chew" on after we read a story. These are the things we ponder and think about in the weeks and months ahead. These are the things God whispers to our hearts as we read the story. Takeaways are also the things God reveals to us in order to change us, teach us or just love on us. And these are the things God brings to mind in the future to help us, guide us or comfort us.

The takeaways at the end of each chapter include Bible verses to support the truth behind each takeaway. The Takeaways listed in each section are not a complete list. Each reader will, more than likely, have their own Takeaways as they read each story and God speaks into their heart.

Chapter 1

Teaching Your Children to Recognize and Know God's Voice

*Direct your children onto the right path,
and when they are older, they will not leave it.*
— Proverbs 22:6 NLT

1995

He was five. It was bedtime. I don't remember the prayers we recited that night, but I do remember the question he asked as I was about to turn out the light…

"Mommy, how does God speak to you?"

I felt my heart skip a beat. His question took me by surprise. I knew the conversation I was about to have with my little boy was one I'd never forget.

"Mommy, God never speaks to me." He explained looking up to me with worried eyes as I returned and knelt at the side of his bed.

How do I explain to a five-year-old how God speaks? I thought to myself, panic filling me as I searched my heart for just the right words. This was a very important conversation and I needed to get it right.

"Michael…Honey…God does speak to you." I continued to struggle to come up with some way to reassure him. "He speaks to all of us."

"But He never speaks to me." My beloved son implored.

The anguish in his little voice brought tears to my eyes and set my heart afire with a new calling. A calling I'd spend the rest of my life fulfilling.

***

The seeds of this book were planted in my heart that night as I knelt next to my child's bedside. Hearing the frustration and yearning in my young son's voice…his desire to know God in an intimate and personal way, sent a shudder through my spirit. What if I couldn't figure out a way to teach him? If I didn't succeed in teaching him, the world would surely direct my son away from God. But, was I even capable of such a task?

To be honest, I'd often had my own doubts as to when God was speaking to me. Who was I to think I could teach my son something I struggled with as an adult?

As I pondered my son's question in the weeks ahead, a heaviness settled into my heart. The ache in his voice…his desperation to hear God's voice…left me little choice. I had to find a way to teach my son to recognize and know God's voice. This was one area in my life where I couldn't afford to fail.

In the years that followed, I took advantage of every opportunity God gave me to talk to my son and daughter about Him. I intentionally gave God credit for things that happened, or didn't happen, in our lives. I tried, best as I could, to frame the events of our lives in a way I thought God might look at them. I shared with my children what I thought might be God's perspective when faced with different challenges or situations. When I felt the Holy Spirit speaking to me, I shared what I thought the Holy Spirit was saying. Even if I was uncertain of how things might turn out, which was pretty much all the time!

At times, teaching my children about God pushed me into a very vulnerable corner. Because, much of the time, I didn't have answers to their questions. In those moments I felt it was important to be real and honest with them. So, I didn't profess to have all the answers. If I didn't have an answer to their question, I told them I didn't have an answer.

As my children grew from being toddlers, to becoming elementary school children, to facing the challenges of high school, college and adulthood, I did my best to teach my children to know the voice of God. But often times, my lack of faith took center stage, as my children watched me wrestle with my own doubt. Who was I to know why God did or didn't do something? Who was I to think I could know the mind of God? I often felt insufficient for the task at hand…unprepared for the calling I felt on my life. But when I stumbled, which was often, God was faithful. All I needed to do was the best I could. I learned I could trust God with the rest.

Somehow…in some way…as I walked the path of parenthood, I knew God would go behind me and put together the parent puzzle pieces I lacked. He would place each piece exactly where it needed to go. And if a piece was missing, God would find it for me, and ensure it found its rightful place in the tapestry of my children's lives.

Early in my journey I came upon the Bible story of Hannah, Eli and Samuel. It confirmed for me the responsibility I had as a parent. The responsibility I had to teach my children to know and recognize the voice of God. The story of Samuel and his amazing mother Hannah strengthened my resolve. It starts out in 1 Samuel 1 and then, years later, continues in 1 Samuel 3.

1 Samuel 1:9-28

Once when they had finished eating and drinking in Shiloh, Hannah stood up. Now Eli the priest was sitting on his chair by the doorpost of the Lord's house. In her deep anguish Hannah prayed to the Lord, weeping bitterly. And she made a vow, saying, "Lord Almighty, if you will only look on your servant's misery and remember me, and not forget your servant but give her a son, then I will give him to the Lord for all the days of his life, and no razor will ever be used on his head."

As she kept on praying to the Lord, Eli observed her mouth. Hannah was praying in her heart, and her lips were moving but her voice was not heard. Eli thought she was drunk and said to her, "How long are you going to stay drunk? Put away your wine."

"Not so, my lord," Hannah replied, "I am a woman who is deeply troubled. I have not been drinking wine or beer; I was pouring out my soul to the Lord. Do not take your servant for a wicked woman; I have been praying here out of my great anguish and grief."

Eli answered, "Go in peace, and may the God of Israel grant you what you have asked of him."

*She said, "May your servant find favor in your eyes."
Then she went her way and ate something, and her face was no longer downcast.*

Early the next morning they arose and worshiped before the Lord and then went back to their home at Ramah. Elkanah made love to his wife Hannah, and the Lord remembered her. So in the course of time Hannah became pregnant and gave birth to a son. She named him Samuel, saying, "Because I asked the Lord for him."

When her husband Elkanah went up with all his family to offer the annual sacrifice to the Lord and to fulfill his vow, Hannah did not go. She said to her husband, "After the boy is weaned, I will take him and present him before the Lord, and he will live there always."

"Do what seems best to you," her husband Elkanah told her. "Stay here until you have weaned him; only may the Lord make good his word." So, the woman stayed at home and nursed her son until she had weaned him.

After he was weaned, she took the boy with her, young as he was, along with a three-year-old bull, an ephah of flour and a skin of wine, and brought him to the house of the Lord at Shiloh. When the bull had been sacrificed, they brought the boy to Eli, and she said to him, "Pardon me, my lord. As surely as you live, I am the woman who stood here beside you praying to the Lord. I prayed for this child, and the Lord has granted me what I asked of him. So now I give him to the Lord. For his whole life he will be given over to the Lord." And he worshiped the Lord there.

1 Samuel 3

The boy Samuel ministered before the Lord under Eli. In those days the word of the Lord was rare; there were not many visions.

One night Eli, whose eyes were becoming so weak that he could barely see, was lying down in his usual place. The lamp of God had not yet gone out, and Samuel was lying down in the house of the Lord, where the ark of God was. Then the Lord called Samuel.

Samuel answered, "Here I am." And he ran to Eli and

said, "Here I am; you called me."

But Eli said, "I did not call; go back and lie down." So, he went and lay down.

Again, the Lord called, "Samuel!" And Samuel got up and went to Eli and said, "Here I am; you called me."

"My son," Eli said, "I did not call; go back and lie down."

Now <u>Samuel did not yet know the Lord: The word of the Lord had not yet been revealed to him.</u>

A third time the Lord called, "Samuel!" And Samuel got up and went to Eli and said, "Here I am; you called me."

<u>Then Eli realized that the Lord was calling the boy.</u> So Eli told Samuel, "Go and lie down, and if he calls you, say, 'Speak, Lord, for your servant is listening.'" So, Samuel went and lay down in his place.

The Lord came and stood there, calling as at the other times, "Samuel! Samuel!"

Then Samuel said, "Speak, for your servant is listening."

And the Lord said to Samuel: "See, I am about to do something in Israel that will make the ears of everyone who hears about it tingle. At that time, I will carry out against Eli everything I spoke against his family—from beginning to end. For I told him that I would judge his family forever because of the sin he knew about; his sons blasphemed God, and he failed to restrain them. Therefore, I swore to the house of Eli, 'The guilt of Eli's house will never be atoned for by sacrifice or offering.'"

Samuel lay down until morning and then opened the doors of the house of the Lord. He was afraid to tell Eli the vision, but Eli called him and said, "<u>Samuel, my son.</u>"

Samuel answered, "Here I am."

"What was it he said to you?" Eli asked. "Do not hide it from me. May God deal with you, be it ever so severely, if you hide from me anything he told you." So, Samuel told him everything, hiding nothing from him. Then Eli said, "He is the Lord; let him do what is good in his eyes."

The Lord was with Samuel as he grew up, and he let none of Samuel's words fall to the ground. And all Israel from Dan to Beersheba recognized that Samuel was attested as a prophet of the Lord. The Lord continued to appear at Shiloh, and there he *revealed himself to Samuel through his word.*

Hannah placed Samuel in the care of Eli when he was a very young child. Eli was technically Samuel's guardian, but Eli called Samuel his son. When the Lord called Samuel's name that night, Samuel didn't recognize God's voice because, according to Scripture, "<u>Samuel did not yet know the Lord: The word of the Lord had not yet been revealed to him.</u>"

It was Eli who had to point out to Samuel that it was the Lord, and not Eli, who had called Samuel's name. In essence, Eli taught Samuel to recognize God's voice.

Parents have this same responsibility. We must teach our children to recognize and know Gods voice.

As parents, we are in a race against the world. If we don't succeed in teaching our children to know God's voice, the world will drown God's voice out. The world will attribute the voice of God to Karma, coincidence, "the universe", a "twist of fate, "your truth", good luck, etc. And eventually, as God's voice is drowned out in the lives of our children, they will be led away from God.

Teaching our children to recognize God's voice is a serious matter. One that cannot be taken lightly. It can mean the difference between your child standing firm on what he/she knows to be true, or your child being lost in darkness unable to find the light of truth.

Proverbs 22:6 NLT says *"Direct your children onto the right path, and when they are older, they will not leave it."*

Parents, this is our call to action! Today we are in the midst of losing the next generation. Heeding this call to action has never been more crucial or more important.

Sharing God Stories with our children is one of the most powerful tools we have when it comes to teaching our children to know God's voice. Jesus taught using stories. Why shouldn't we do the same?

This book is filled with stories of events that took place in the lives of my family and myself. These stories have been told and retold many times.

You also have stories God has written into your life. Isn't it time to dust off the pages of your memory and share your God

Stories with your children?

A Mother's Thoughts

I once had a family member who became frustrated with me during a conversation.

"Why do you always have to bring God into everything? Can't we just have a conversation without you talking about, or bringing up God?"

Until that moment I hadn't thought much about how I spoke and the references I often made about God when I talked to people. Talking about God in my conversations with others was as natural to me as breathing. My loved one's question caused me to pause and think hard before I answered.

"For me, talking about God is like talking about my children or my husband," I explained to her.

"Yes, I can have a conversation with you without bringing up God," I surmised. "I can talk to you about the weather, I can ask you how your day was, or we could talk about things like shopping, the news or whatever...but our conversations wouldn't have any depth to them. Our conversations would be very shallow interactions between the two of us...And I can do that," I assured her. "But if you really want to know me on a personal level and have a close relationship with me, then no, I can't exclude God."

"God is like another person in our family." I continued to explain to her as honestly as I could. "He is the fifth seat at our dinner table every night. God is as real and present to me as my children, my husband and all the other people in my life that I love deeply."

"I can't honestly share my life with you on a personal level, and have a close relationship with you, without sharing about my family and the people I love...and that includes God." I tried to help her understand.

Talking to our children (and others) about God is something we must intentionally choose to do. Initially it may feel awkward or even a bit uncomfortable. But we must overcome our fear and hesitation. The more we talk about God, the easier it becomes. Like I explained to my loved one, when you have a relationship with God, talking about Him is much like breathing. And it becomes impossible to exclude Him in our conversations.

Teaching our children to know God's voice is a lifelong calling. It's not a "one and done" sort of deal. If you take this calling seriously, it will impact every area of our life.

On the next few pages is the beginning of a list of 11 suggestions that will help get you started. I say it's a "beginning" because I don't profess to have all the answers. I, too, continue to learn as I grow in my faith.

These 11 suggestions are things I've implemented in my own life as a mother and grandmother. They are things that have helped me as I've stumbled through trying to do my best to teach my children to know God. I hope they will help you on your journey as you heed the call and teach your child to recognize and know God's voice.

Teaching Your Children to Recognize and Know God's Voice

1) **Point out "God Sightings" in the lives of your children, whenever an opportunity presents itself.**
   Point out, in real time, when you see God working in your life or your child's life.

2) **Journal the "God Stories" of your life.**
   Record the many ways in which God has spoken to you and revealed Himself to you. It's so easy for us to forget all God has done in our lives. It's time to write the stories down. If you do this, not only will you be able to share your stories with your loved ones today, but you will leave a legacy of God's work in your life that will be read and shared, long after you depart this world.

3) **Boldly, in faith, share your God Stories.**
Share the God Stories of today, as well as those in the dust of your past. Think back and remember what God has done in your life. And share your stories, even if you are still waiting for God to answer a prayer from long ago. In the "Mother's Thoughts" section of each chapter, I often share some of the ways in which God has spoken to me or those in my family. My hope is that, as you reflect back on your own stories, you will be able to see how God has also spoken to you. This will lay the foundation for you to be able to teach your own children how to recognize and know God's voice.

4) **Share your doubt in real time.**
We all doubt from time to time. It's important to share our faith, and lack of it, with our children. Share the times when God answers your prayers, but more importantly, share the times when you are waiting for an answer from God. If our children can watch and wait with us, as we wait on God, they too will experience Him. They too will see how faithful God is to those who call upon Him and trust Him.

5) **Pray for God to put a hedge of protection around your children every day.**
We cannot be with our children 24/7. Our children are under spiritual attack in most every area of their lives. At school, watching television, movies, at friends' houses, etc. Don't be surprised if the assault on your children escalates as you read this book and start to apply these principles to your life.

That is how Satan responds when we reach out to God. In the Bible, in the Book of Job, Satan recognized the hedge of protection God had placed around Job.
Have you not put a hedge around him and his household and everything he has? You have blessed the work of his hands, so that his flocks and herds are spread throughout the land. - Job 1:10

Hedges of protection are real in the spirit world and God can and will answer your prayer to put a hedge of protection around your children.

6) **Pray that God will reveal Himself to your child.**
Pray that God will reveal Himself in ways in which your child will be able to grasp who God is, how God works and how God speaks.

7) **Live a life of gratefulness.**
The way we live our lives, and the way we talk about our lives, speaks volumes to our children. Live a life that consistently sees the glass as half full, not half empty. Speak to your children constantly about the blessings God pours into your life every day. Speak using words that edify your grateful and thankful heart.

8) **Pray over your children.**
Constantly. Pray for your children both privately, and out loud in their presence. Intentionally let your children hear you talk to God about them.

9) **Speak of God as your companion.**
Because He is. He is a constant and near companion. He is never distant. If your children see God as your companion, they will be able to embrace Him as their companion.

10) **Ask God to teach you.**
I often pray, *Lord, teach me, to teach my child, to know Your voice.* God promises to give wisdom to those who ask. If there has ever been a time in history when we've needed wisdom, it most certainly is today.

11) **And most importantly, pray that your child will fall head over heels in love with God.**
Love should be our motive when we pursue a relationship with God. I've often felt that if my children would fall deeply in love with God, I'd be able to lay aside so many of the concerns I have for their lives. It stands to reason that if

my children love God with their entire heart, soul and mind, then that love will be a compass in their lives that will always keep them on course.

Take Aways

1. **Parents and grandparents are called to teach their children.**
   These commandments that I give you today are to be on your hearts. Impress them on your children. Talk about them when you sit at home and when you walk along the road, when you lie down and when you get up.
   - Deuteronomy 6:6-7

   Start children off on the way they should go, and even when they are old, they will not turn from it. - Proverbs 22:6

2. **God commands that we tell (the stories of what God has done) to our children and to their children after them.**
   Only be careful, and watch yourselves closely so that you do not forget the things your eyes have seen or let them fade from your heart as long as you live. Teach them to your children and to their children after them.
   - Deuteronomy 4:9

3. **God can, and will, surround you and your children with a hedge of protection. Ask Him.**
   Have you not put a hedge (of protection) around him and his household and everything he has? You have blessed the work of his hands, so that his flocks and herds are spread throughout the land. - Job 1:10

Chapter 2

God Speaks Through Answered Prayer

If you abide in me, and my words abide in you, ask whatever You wish, and it will be done for you. – John 15:7 ESV

August 1975

Mom met me in Montreal at the end of the summer to drive me home after a long week of racing. Several of our teams from Camp Ak-O-Mak, spent the first week of August competing in the 1975 Canadian National Paddling Championships. The championship took place in Montreal, Canada on the soon to be completed 1976 Olympic Site. I'd raced in four events over the week and had done well. I'd even medaled in a few races.

Once I returned to Michigan, word of my success in Canada traveled quickly. My family and friends are now telling me I should try out for the Olympics. Mom is at the root of most of the talk and she isn't helpful in quelling the chatter. She loves touting my accomplishments to anyone who will lend an ear and as a result, everyone I know, now has a bad case of Olympic fever.

Although I did well at nationals, I'm nowhere near ready for the Olympics. But the drum beat of those around me is loud and constant. As a result, I've actually started wondering if God is trying to tell me something. Perhaps He wants me to try out for the Olympics?

The other day, when mom and I drove into town to run some errands, I sought mom's advice.

"Mom, everyone is telling me I should try out for the Olympics, but that's unrealistic and pretty much impossible." Mom is silent as I continue. "But it does make me wonder if maybe God is behind all the talk. So, I decided to ask God to give me a sign if He wants me to try out for the Olympics."

Mom laughs and shakes her head, "Renee, you have such a blind faith! If it was me, I'd ask God for a sign that is much more specific. But not you! You just ask God to give you a sign…any sign!" She's a bit mystified at how I'm handling my dilemma and offers a suggestion. "Maybe you should ask God for something more specific in terms of a sign?"

I think about her suggestion for a split second.

"Nope, I already prayed." My stubbornness dismisses the idea. "I already asked Him. If God wants me to try out for the Olympics, He'll give me a sign."

***

Kicking the stones in my path aside, I entered the driveway having just returned from my friend's house who lived on the other side of the lake. We'd gotten into an argument so I'd left his house and walked home early.

What a rotten day! Nothing is going right since I got home from nationals.

"Renee, Renee!" My little sister yells as she runs up the long dirt driveway of our lakefront cottage. "Stan told dad about your paddle!"

Great. Just what I need. Can today get any worse?

"How do you know that?" I wonder if she's mistaken.

"I heard him telling dad." She looks as nervous as I feel.

Well, that seals the deal!

Now I'd have to find my father and tell him about the paddle. Fear of what he'll say or do has kept me from sharing my secret with him for the last week. But now I'm backed into a corner and I have no choice.

I guess there's no time like the present to come clean and face the music…I think defeated…this isn't going to end well…he's going to be furious.

I find my father in the garage working on a motor at his work bench.

"Dad?" My dad's back is facing me but I have to make sure he hears my entire story. Telling him the first time is going to be hard, but if I have to repeat myself a second time…well, that would be brutal.

"Yup." Dad glances over his shoulder and continues working on the motor in front of him.

"I have something I need to tell you." I try to steady my voice and get ready for what is about to happen.

"Ok." Dad grunts, continuing to work.

"When I was at nationals, I bought a paddle." My mouth shifts into warp speed. I can't get my words out fast enough.

"Mom paid for it but I promised her I'd ask you for the money when I got home so I could pay her back. I bought it so that I can have my own paddle at camp next summer. I really need my own paddle, Dad. It'll be so much nicer not having to share paddles with all the other girls..." I finally stop. Out of breath.

Dad is silent. It's probably less than ten seconds, but it feels like forever before he answers.

"I'll tell you what." He responds from behind his back.

"What?" I swallow hard preparing myself for a bucket load of anger that is about to be thrown my way...and yet something is amiss...

This is different...he doesn't seem mad...he usually gets really mad when I ask him for money...

"If you try out for the 1976 Olympics, I'll pay for that paddle." Dad responds calmly and picks up the screw driver to tighten a bolt on the top of the motor.

"What?!" I take a step back not understanding what's happening. Surely, he doesn't understand. "Dad, that's not possible. I've only been paddling for a total of six months of my entire life. I know I did well at nationals, but people don't try out for the Olympics after only six months of training." I give my father a sideways glance. I still can't believe he's not angry. Anger I can deal with. Anger is something I've had practice dealing with, but this?

"Well, that's the deal." He responds as he lifts the motor up to the light from the window to get a better view.

Dad has always been absent in our lives. He comes to very few school or sporting events. Mom's always the one in the stands rooting us kids on. I'm surprised dad has any knowledge of how I've done at nationals.

And now he's playing "Let's Make a Deal" with me? I laugh to myself. *This can't be happening...*

Given the fact that my father's presence in my life has been pretty much nonexistent, the deal Dad is now suggesting is quite a big deal to me.

"Dad, that's not possible! Olympic Trials are less than a year away. There's no way I have time to prepare for something like that. How about 1980? How about I try out in 1980?" I counter.

"Nope." He finally turns and faces me. "1976."

"Dinner's ready!" Mom yells from the kitchen.

Dad sets down the motor and wipes the grease off his hands using the rag sitting on his work bench. He and I continue to banter about his deal as we make our way out of the garage and into the kitchen.

"Mom, did you hear what dad just said?' I laugh walking into the kitchen, doubting my father is serious.

"No, what did he say?" She glances toward me as she takes the dinner casserole out of the oven.

"Dad said if I try out for next year's Olympics he'll pay for my paddle." I laugh, still finding it hard to believe this conversation is taking place. "But that's ridiculous. There's no way I can try out next year."

Mom sets the casserole on the stove and turns to me with a gotcha smile, "Well, you asked for a sign." She laughs out loud with a twinkle in her eye. Mom's response catches me off guard.

"That's not the sign." I spout back, remembering our conversation from earlier in the week. There is no way my mom is right about this.

Mom laughs again as she takes a knife and starts cutting the casserole into pieces.

"Like I said…you asked for a sign." She giggles to herself clearly amused by the turn of events.

***

The next day, after returning home from the cottage, I think a lot about the conversations I'd had with dad and mom.

Perhaps this is God's sign? I surmise. *Maybe God really*

is telling me to do this? But how? I have nothing!

Sitting on my bed after unpacking my suitcase, I'm so torn and so confused. I want to do what God wants me to do, but if trying out for the Olympics is what God is telling me to do, then I have no idea how to do it!

My beautiful paddle standing proudly in the corner of my bedroom catches my eye. The different wood grains and colors that make up each blade are exquisite. Made in Hungary, the craftsmanship of my paddle is magnificent. Its beauty makes me smile and causes a warm stirring in my heart.

"God, if this is the sign...the one I asked You for...I'll try out for the Olympics if You want me to."

There. I finally said it.

"But God, all I have is this paddle. I don't have a kayak. And I don't have a coach."

I'm sure God is beginning to see how ridiculous this whole idea of trying out for the Olympics is.

"Lord, the Olympic Trials are less than seven months away...not a whole lot of time to train!" I continue to present my case to God.

If I haven't already persuaded God that I'm right about this, I figure I'll give Him a few more points to consider.

Renee and her paddle.

"Heck! It'll be winter soon! There's no place to paddle in Michigan in the winter! Just think about that...even if I did have a boat to paddle, in a few months I'll have nowhere to paddle it!"

I laugh to myself confidently dismissing the idea. I doubt God is telling me to train for the Olympic Trials.

But as I continue to wrestle with my thoughts, a feeling of humility slowly seeps into my heart. I lean forward and cover my face with my hands struggling with my emotions.

Slowly the tears come...and start to trickle through my

fingers. I desperately want to know what God wants me to do. And I want to do what He wants me to do. But if I'm honest with myself, I'm also afraid of what He might be asking me to do.

"All I have is a paddle, Lord." I remind Him in a whisper through my tears. "But if You want me to try out for the 1976 Olympics, I'll do it…if You'll supply the rest."

September 1975

Dad moved out of the house a few weeks ago. Our parents never really sat us kids down and told us. But we've figured it out. They are getting a divorce.

Our life together as a family is beginning to unravel. Phone call after phone call. Fight after fight. Piece by piece our whole world is slowly being destroyed.

It feels like someone has pulled the rug of my life out from underneath me. And I'm in a frightening, uncontrollable free fall not knowing if, or where, I'll land.

I have so many emotions and feelings running through me. Fear is the most prominent. Unbearable pain is a close second. Both are beyond my control.

A deep depression has settled into my soul. I hurt so bad. I'm not sure how to live with this pain. I don't think I can. I have to find a way to escape this unending, unbearable pain. But there is no escape.

Thoughts of suicide taunt me every day. Suicide might be my only answer to the crushing hurt that's slowly suffocating the life out of me. Suicide would be peaceful. It is starting to become my fantasy.

As the oldest of seven, I now feel a heightened sense of responsibility for each of my brothers and sisters. I also feel responsible for my mother. She's struggling. She's drinking more. A lot more. As a result, I've taken on the role of her pseudo parent. But there's nothing within my control that I can do to help myself, my mother or my siblings. I am powerless.

Mom now has the responsibility of raising all seven of us. I'm 17. My youngest brother is two. Mom works full time. She's as emotionally shredded as the rest of us. She only has enough strength to try to deal with her own pain. And she's visibly failing at that. She has nothing to give us.

My siblings and I can't even help one another. Our personal battles consume everything within us. Leaving nothing. Each of us must somehow find our own way out of this darkness.

My high school friends are concerned about me. They whisper. They never know who is coming to school each day. The old me...or the new dark me. They watch as I sleep walk through the suffocating darkness that is now my life. They worry. I don't share my dark thoughts with them...or the solution I've come up with to end my pain. But my friends sense the danger I'm in. They try to make me laugh. They try to engage me in high school shenanigans and funny conversations to take my mind off things. Sometimes they're successful at distracting me. Sometimes I smile and a flutter of warmth finds its way into the coldness within me. But no matter how hard my friends try to help, anything they do is only a temporary reprieve. The darkness always pushes its way back in. My friends are powerless to help.

October 1975

The phone rings as I'm helping mom get dinner on the table. Mom answers the rotary phone in the kitchen after waiting the required two rings. A few minutes later she calls my name.

"Renee, phone for you." She smiles with a hint of mischief in her eyes and extends the phone receiver in my direction.

I take the phone from her while silently mouthing a question. *Who's on the phone?*

"Hello?" I answer. Still looking at Mom who ignored my question with a smirk on her face.

"Hi Renee, this is Connie." My mind boomerangs back to the caller. Mom laughs out loud as she watches the shockwave move across my face.

I take a minute to absorb the impact of the caller's identity before speaking.

Connie is ten years my senior and the daughter of Camp Ak-O-Mak's Executive Directors, Buck and RoseMary Dawson. Connie is the best kayak paddler at camp and someone all of us younger paddlers pretty much idolize.

My camp friends and I have spent many a summer afternoon sitting on the dock at camp watching Connie and her partner Robin race their boat across the waters of Ahmic Lake in Ontario, Canada. Connie and Robin are senior paddlers with so much experience. And they are so successful. My friends and I doubt we'll ever come close to being as good as Connie and Robin. I had no idea Connie even knew my name, much less my phone number.

Why on earth is she calling ME?

"Hi Connie." I answer confused and star struck at the same time.

"Renee, have you ever dreamed of trying out for the Olympics?" Connie's question makes my heart stop. Mom laughs at the fact that my mouth is now hanging wide open. She is clearly enjoying the show!

Before I can answer Connie shares how she wants me to be her partner and compete in the 1976 Olympic Trials in Ohio in May. She tells me she's arranged for the kayaks from camp to be transported to her Ft. Lauderdale, Florida home. And she's lined up a coach and a place for me to stay.

"You'd have to complete your final semester of your senior year down here in Florida." Connie explains to me, confident of her plan. "I checked with the high school down here. They're willing to let you go to school here and transfer your credits back to Michigan at the end of the semester. But you'd have to ask your school if they'd let you do that."

Connie has obviously put a lot of time and thought into this.

"I know this is a big decision," she continues. "You probably need some time to think about it. I don't need an answer right now. Take a week or so to think about it and call me back. I really want you to be my partner."

My head is spinning. Connie has everything I need to fulfill the promise I made to God two months ago.

Is this really happening?!
Wow! HOW can this be happening?
What am I supposed to say?!

I gather some words together in my mind to reply to her

the best I can.

"Connie, you aren't going to believe this, but I committed to doing this two months ago." I then fill Connie in on how I'd prayed and asked God for a sign, the story about my dad and his deal, and how I'd told God I'd try out for the Olympics if He provided everything I needed.

"Well, take some time to think about it and let me know." Connie repeats. I'm not sure she believes what I've just confessed to.

A few minutes later Connie and I say our goodbyes and I absentmindedly return the receiver to the phone cradle.

Getting my school to agree will be the final hurdle. The school's "yes", means I'll be moving to Florida in January.

***

The next day Mom and I talk to my high school counselor about taking classes in Florida and transferring credits back to Michigan so I can graduate in June with my high school classmates. East Grand Rapids High School is more than happy to support me in my endeavors. Within a few weeks after the phone call, everything is in place for me to make the move to Florida.

Mom and I call Connie and give her the good news.

"That's wonderful!" She's so excited it's all worked out. "I'll talk to the school here in Ft Lauderdale and set everything up on my end. Plan on coming down right after the new year. Your room will be ready!"

Getting ready to leave for Florida sets off a whirlwind of events. There's so much to do and I have little time to think about anything else. God has suddenly redirected my focus and changed the path of my life.

January 1976

I arrive in Florida just after the new year and settle into my new home with Connie, her sister and her parents. My bedroom is the screened in porch on the back of their house. The porch sits alongside a canal where Connie and I will launch our kayaks every day. The mild weather in Florida makes my new bedroom a very comfortable living space.

Renee and Connie practicing on the canals throughout the intercoastal waterway in Fort Lauderdale, Florida.

Connie and I spend every day training on the intercoastal waterways that run throughout Ft Lauderdale, Florida. Most days we train twice a day. I only need three classes to graduate high school, which means I only have to go to school in the morning. That gives me the rest of the day to train with Connie.

The time goes by quickly as Connie and I train hard week after week. With each week that passes, the two of us become more and more confident in, not only our partnership, but in our chances of making the 1976 United States Olympic Kayaking Team.

February 1976

Every day I wonder where God is leading me. Where and how will this journey end? I know God is behind everything that's happening to me right now. Knowing this gives me a warm peace and confidence, and helps keep me going.

Mom calls me from Michigan at least once a week. The divorce is making its way through the court system. Mom calls to ask my advice on what she should do. Recently she asked my opinion regarding what properties she should ask for in the divorce settlement.

I do my best to advise my mom, but being put in the middle, between her and my father, makes me feel uncomfortable. I also feel strangely disconnected. It's hard trying to help her when I'm so far away.

Sometimes I feel guilty about the fact that I no longer have to live on the front lines of that unbearable pain. There's so much space between me and what's happening at home and the distance has provided me an escape from the darkness. I like being able to breathe again. I like that my heart lays in a soft blanket of protection and safety and my mind no longer wrestles with dark thoughts.

During the months leading up to the trials I continue to take advantage of every opportunity God gives me to tell my story to those God puts in my path. Sometimes I feel foolish because I have no idea how this journey will end. Will Connie and I make the Olympic Team after only four months of paddling together? That seems impossible! But it would be a miracle if it happened! I have no idea what God will do at the trials in May. The only thing I know for certain is that God brought me to Florida for a purpose and my job is to do the best I can with what He's given me.

A Mother's Thoughts

Many years later, as I reflected back on my senior year in high school, I realized what the call from Connie in October of 1975 had really been about.

God's plan was never about the Olympics. It was about God intervening…it was about God saving me.

I'm not sure I'd have survived living at home while my parents were going through their divorce. I don't know where I'd be today had God not intervened. He saw my struggle. He felt my pain and He knew what He had to do to save me. And so, He did.

God put together a plan to move aside the mountains to make a way for the impossible. No boat? No problem. No coach? No problem. No place to paddle? No problem. God scooped up all the pieces of my shattered life, picked me up and put me back together in a safe place a few thousand miles away. And in doing so, He gave me a new purpose and focus. The Olympics.

During my time in Florida, I went through an emotional and spiritual transformation of sorts. I joined a church and took the steps necessary to be confirmed in my faith. At church God connected me with some very special people who helped strengthen my faith. As a result, I became stronger and more confident in who I was.

In January I'd left Michigan as a very insecure, hurting teenager, and four months later, I returned home as a confident young adult with a brand-new outlook, ready to live life.

Connie and I ended up placing 8th at the Olympic Trials. In order to make the United States Olympic Team we would have had to place 1st or 2nd. For some reason, I wasn't disappointed in our finish. We gave it our best shot and I know, without a doubt, that God was in our 8th place finish.

Not making the Olympic Team was God's perfect will for our lives. And I will always be thankful for the incredible experience God gave me as a young hurting teenage girl. It truly was the adventure of a lifetime.

Today, even after all these years, God continues to give me opportunities to tell the story of Connie and I, and the Olympics. When people cross paths with me and hear the word "Olympics", they're naturally curious. They want to hear what happened. It's incredible how God still uses this timeless story to touch the lives of so many people, in so many different ways. And I never tire of telling the story because each time I tell it I am reminded of one hidden truth…from God's vantage point, Connie and I really did win the race of our lives.

Take Aways

1. God speaks through prayer.
   If you abide in me, and my words abide in you, ask whatever you wish, and it will be done for you.
   - John 15:7 ESV

2. God speaks through supplying what we need.
   And my God will supply every need of yours according to his riches in glory in Christ Jesus.   - Philippians 4:19 ESV

3. God speaks through his Holy Spirit, who dwells within every believer.
   When the Spirit of Truth comes, he will guide you into all the truth, for he will not speak on his own authority, but whatever he hears me will speak, and he will declare to you the things that are to come. – John 16:13 ESV

4. God, though our faith, can and will, move mountains for us.
   And Jesus answered them, "Truly, I say to you, if you have faith and do not doubt, you will not only do what has been done to the fig tree, but even if you say to this mountain, 'Be taken up and thrown into the sea,' it will happen. - Matthew 21:21 ESV

5. God loves us and protects us. He will never, ever leave us.
   Fear not, for I am with you; be not dismayed, for I am your God; I will strengthen you, I will help you, I will uphold you with my righteous hand. - Isaiah 41:10 ESV

6. God knows what was, what is and what will be.
   Nothing that happens to us comes as a surprise to God. All the days of our lives were written before one of them came to be.

   You made all the delicate, inner parts of my body and knit me together in my mother's womb. Thank you for making me so wonderfully complex! Your workmanship is marvelous—how well I know it. You watched me as I was being formed in utter seclusion, as I was woven together in the dark of the womb. You saw me before I was born. Every day of my life was recorded in your book. Every moment was laid out before a single day had passed.
   - Psalm 139:1

Chapter 3

God Speaks in A Still, Small Voice

And after the earthquake there was a fire, but the LORD was not in the fire. And after the fire there was the sound of a gentle whisper.
- 1 Kings 19:12

October 18, 1988

It's a chilly, dark morning on the streets of Windsor, Ontario. My husband Mike and brother Stacy dropped me off at the starting line in Jackson Park well before the 7:00 a.m. start time. After saying goodbye and wishing me luck, they've headed back across the Canadian-United States border to search for a place to stand along the crowded race route. They hope to secure a spot on a curb somewhere in downtown Detroit where they can yell encouragement, and maybe take a few pictures of me, when I run past later today.

I'm not sure how today will go. Although I'm an avid runner, I've only trained a grand total of three weeks for this marathon. It's ridiculous to think I'll even come close to making it to the finish line today. But a strange inner peace fills me. A peace that God covered me in at the beginning of this journey.

At the moment I'm standing in the park in a crowd of accomplished long-distance runners. And I don't know a soul. If I give it much thought, it's easy to feel intimidated. But the peace that covers my heart is steadfast. Training or not, I'm ready to run this race. I have no idea what I'll encounter along the way, but I'm as ready as I'll ever be. And truth be told, today isn't really about this race…today is more about the journey…or maybe it's about an escape…today is about finding a door that will lead me back into the land of the living.

I pull my knit cap down over my ears and blow into my hands to keep warm. Jumping up and down helps keep me from getting chilled. And shaking out my arms and legs helps keep my blood flowing. There are amazing runners all around me. I don't want anyone to think I don't know what I'm doing...or that I've never done this before.

I should probably stretch. I reason with myself. *Yes, stretching would be a good idea.*

Finding a tree to help myself balance, I lean forward and begin to stretch out my calves.

26.2 miles. My mind stumbles over the number causing my body to tip to one side.

I've never come close to running 26.2 miles before. Not in one run anyways. A week ago, I made it 13 miles in a training run...but 13 miles is only half of what is expected today.

Prior to today I've never even run a race, much less a marathon. Finishing this race, on what little training I have, is likely impossible. Thus, the reason I've kept my entry into the race, a secret from most everyone I know. I don't need anyone telling me I can't do this. I don't need anyone confirming that I'm about to embark on the impossible. I KNOW it's pretty much impossible. But I have to do this. My life is riding on it. And besides, I have little options left. The results at the end of today, will likely determine life or death for me.

I know that...And God knows that...But no one else has any idea what's riding on today.

I take comfort in the fact that I know God is the one who led me here today. Without Him I wouldn't be here embarking on the impossible.

God, please help me do this. I can't do this on my own.

Standing up I take an accounting of the sea of runners around me, their faces partially hidden by little puffs of fog created by the warmth of their breath. Thousands of runners. All preparing for 26.2 miles of the unknown.

What I am doing here? Doubt begins a slow crawl into my psyche.

Is there anyone here like me who has only trained for a few weeks? I chuckle to myself.

Doubtful. My dry sense of humor helps lift some of my anxiety.

Sleep evaded me last night. A string of nightmares showcased a series of possible tragic endings for today. Thankfully, by morning, the night terrors were washed away and my heart was filled anew with hope and an anticipation of the adventure ahead. As I continue my survey of this impressive group of runners, I feel God's presence around me. I have no idea what He's about to do, but I can sense Him in the middle of all of this. And I'm reminded...*but God.* Had it not been for Him, I wouldn't be here. He's the One who whispered to my heart to enter this race.

I place my hands back on the tree. Right foot forward, left foot back and try hard to stretch out the anxiety. Closing my eyes, I can't help but think back to the last few months...and wish my life was somehow different...

Mike and I have been separated for months. Our marriage is in trouble. Deep trouble. It's a teetering on the edge of a cliff sort of trouble. As a result, Depression has slithered its way into my mind like an unwelcome snake that has taken up residence in my soul. Depression's fingers have had a death grip on my heart for weeks slowly squeezing out what little desire I have left for life while, at the same time, luring me toward The Pit.

I've escaped The Pit once before. It's an abyss where Depression makes the convincing case that suicide is my only option...my only escape from the unbearable pain that has a stranglehold on my heart.

My old nemesis Depression always fights dirty...really dirty. And lately I've grown weary. Very weary. I'm weary of fighting Depression and I'm weary of the constant daily struggle of trying to keep my head up above the murky waters of my life. I've been holding on by a thread and I'm desperate to free myself from Depression's death grip.

Opening my eyes, I switch legs and shake my head to rid myself of the dark thoughts. I put my left foot forward and right foot back to stretch out my right calf. The past few weeks of training for this marathon have temporarily ushered Depression to the sidelines of my life. Depression's absence, along with the peace God has given me, has enabled me to use what little time I've had in the last few weeks to focus on preparing for this race.

Looking up I scan the crowd again hoping to see a familiar face. Today is the 10th running of the *Detroit Free Press International Marathon*. A marathon that draws runners from all over the world. Electricity is in the air and anticipation is growing stronger with each passing minute. Hope is alive along with a certainty that records will be broken today. Personal records and professional records. Best times will be beat and even shattered. As a result, many dreams are about to come true.

I feel totally out of place, and completely out of my element.

Who am I to think I can even come close to running 26.2 miles? I laugh to myself.

But this race holds out hope to me too. Hope that God will show up in a big way. Hope that today will be the day, when the power Depression has over my life, will finally be destroyed forever.

God doesn't care. Depression whispers in an evil, sinister voice interrupting my thoughts.

But God... I counter with all the confidence I can muster. *I know God cares...He showed me a few weeks ago...*

It was a Friday. Mike had stopped by. Even though we were living apart, he'd been stopping by pretty frequently of late. Probably to check in on me. I think he sensed Depression's presence around me. And regardless of our talks about getting a divorce, I think Mike still cared.

It was in the late afternoon when the doorbell rang. I wiped away the tears before I opened the door to find Mike standing on the front porch of my rented duplex.

"Hey." He smiled in greeting taking note of my red, swollen eyes. "The salmon are running. Stacy and I are going up to the cottage to fish on the river. We're wondering if you want to come along?"

His obvious concern for me softened my heart. I looked down at the porch floorboards to avert the unasked question I saw in his eyes as I considered his invitation.

A change of scenery might do me good. Being at my family's cottage had always had a calming effect on me. So many of my most wonderful memories lived at the lake where I spent my childhood weekends. Maybe a visit would help lighten my dark mood. Besides, I'd probably be by myself most of the time because when Mike and Stacy went fishing, they always spent the entire day down on the river.

I looked up and met the concern in Mike's eyes. "Sure, why not." I replied offering a small smile.

Mike, Stacy and I left a few hours later. The 90-minute drive north was gorgeous. It was the perfect autumn day in Michigan and the trees lining the rural highway were stunning.

Looking out the van window as the three of us sped north, I was reminded of what a magnificent artist God is. A tapestry of reds, yellows and oranges splashed across the horizon in a spectacular display of magnificence as we covered the miles leading to Baldwin, Michigan. The colors God had chosen for the day were vibrant, varied and breathtaking. I found the intense beauty of God's artistry both magical and inspiring.

We arrived at the cottage late in the evening, just in time for the guys to organize their fishing gear, tie up their lines and get to bed. It would be an early morning for them. The race to get to the best fishing hole would begin well before day break. Hopefully they'd be in the river, with their lines in the water before the sleepy fishermen in the nearby cabins rolled out of bed.

As we settled in for the night, Mike and I walked to opposite sides of the cottage to our separate bedrooms. A fishing invitation and a beautiful car ride north hadn't lessened the distance between us.

***

Early the next morning the guys tumbled out of bed before the alarm clock rang, anxious to get to the riverbank. Foregoing breakfast, they packed up their gear and left before the light of day. The race was on. They were anxious to find their spot on the river, get their lines in the water and settle in for the day. Sacrificing a bit of sleep was worth eating salmon for supper.

I awoke mid-morning to the sweet sound of a robin's song outside my window. It was going to be an unusually warm day. One of those glorious Indian summer days.

Getting out of bed I put on my favorite raggedy, old sweatshirt over my pajama top and stepped into my slippers. The wonderful smell of water beckoned me to the back porch where the glorious view from the hillside was as wonderful as I remembered. I looked out over the horizon and breathed in the beauty and the memories.

I love this place. I sighed and smiled to myself.

Water always had a calming effect on me. I loved the smell of it…the sound of it…and the sight of it. It felt so good to be at my home away from home.

Walking back inside I went into the kitchen to make coffee and think about the day ahead. I had the whole day to myself.

What should I do today?

The last week had been a long and busy one at work. It felt good to be able to slow down and get away from the rat race. Maybe I'd read a book or take a long walk in the woods. Anything to clear my mind.

The coffee maker beeped twice signaling my coffee was ready. I found a cup in the cupboard and filled it, before making my way back to the living room. Sitting down on the sofa I leaned back into the well-worn cushions and let out a sigh as I looked around the room. Since my parent's divorce, the family memories that now filled this place, triggered a mixed bag of emotions within me. Some good, some not so good. The feelings that erupted inside my heart from the memories, made me wonder if the pain in my heart would ever completely disappear? Would I ever again feel that life, and the pain that often comes with it, was worth living?

I blinked my eyes, shook my head and took a sip of the dark brown liquid in an attempt to chase away the questions that began to flood into my heart. Such dark thoughts to have on such a beautiful morning.

My attention was drawn to the Sunday newspaper laying on the coffee table in front of me. An article about a training run for the *Detroit Free Press Marathon* caught my eye. A picture of a woman on the front page of the sports section pricked my curiosity. Sitting up, I set down my mug on the coffee table to take a closer look. The woman in the picture ran a training run yesterday in preparation for an upcoming marathon. Something in my spirit softly began to stir as I continued to read.

The marathon would take place in Detroit in three weeks. *Run.*

The whisper from my heart brought tears to my eyes…and I sensed God's presence.

Run this marathon? Is that what you're saying God? I chuckled through unshed tears. *Impossible! No one runs 26.2 miles without doing some very intensive training.*

Run. The still, small voice repeated.

It takes a lot of time to train for a marathon. I argued back. *And this marathon is only three weeks away.*

It had been weeks since I'd put on my shoes and felt like running. Depression had stolen so much from me in the last month.

But maybe I can do this. The idea began to take hold. What do I have to lose?

God is this really what You want me to do?...or is this just me having crazy thoughts?

I picked up my coffee and blew across the top of the cup as I pondered the idea being laid out before me.

I think God is really telling me to do this. I thought to myself.

But how? Hope began to fill me as a new confidence broke ground in the emptiness within me.

Why not? I asked myself looking out the window just as a flock of geese landed on the water on the far side of the lake.

As the geese called out to one another in greeting, a smile began to slowly paint itself on my face… *This is crazy!...*I thought enjoying the smile… the first real smile I'd experienced in weeks.

The memory fades as I turn my attention back to the race ahead. The race would start soon. The weather was getting warmer. It was going to be a perfect day for running.

Yep...I AM crazy! I chuckle to myself. *Just crazy enough to think I can really do this.*

A voice on the loud speaker interrupts my thoughts. The race director announces that the runners would start in waves, two minutes apart. Having so many runners, means that most of us would actually start running the race well before the starting line.

What's a few more steps? My sense of humor makes an attempt at taking away my fear.

The director explains that the fastest runners need to move to the front of the pack. It's important for them to start the race at the actual starting line so their finish times are accurate. In a little while I'll go in search of a starting position closer to the back of the pack.

I continue stretching to calm my nerves. Grabbing my right foot, I swing it behind me to stretch out my right quad. My leg muscles scream in protest at my choice of daybreak for a run.

I wonder what God will do today? I can't believe I'm actually starting to look forward to running 26.2 miles. I review my race strategy in my head as the director begins the count down to the start of the race.

I'm not really here to race. I remind myself. *I'm here to finish. I'll just take it slow and pace myself.* I tell myself before an awareness of someone watching me interrupts my thoughts.

A middle-aged man stretching nearby nods hello as I turn to see who is watching me. "Perfect day for a race!" He calls from across the park.

"A bit chilly right now but it's warming up." I stop stretching and turn to him with a curious smile. "Where you from?"

"The UP." His response is a dead giveaway he's from Michigan. UP is slang for the most northern part of Michigan...the Upper Peninsula.

"Where you from?" He asks in return.

I hold up my hand and point to the middle of my palm. "Middle of the mitten. Near Midland."

He nods in acknowledgment. "Funny how us Michiganders use our hands to show where we live." He laughs. "I'm not familiar with your part of the state. I don't get down here very often," he shares, referring to the lower peninsula.

Then he asks me the one question everyone is asking one another this morning. "Ever run a marathon?"

"Nope. First Time." I respond a bit shaken. For some reason, saying it out loud somehow makes it all seem a lot more real. As soon as the words tumble out of my mouth, my second guessing begins.

Can I really do this?

"That's awesome!" The man smiles broadly giving me a thumbs up. "How long you been training for?"

"Three weeks." I reply anxiously awaiting his response. The expression on his face assures me he's now mentally calculating the number of weeks I've been training.

His calculation complete, he stops stretching, stands up and turns to me.

"Really?" He asks hoping for more information.

"How long you been training for?" I ask trying to deflect his question.

"About a year." His eyes betray his curiosity. "Not a lot of people I know run a marathon after only three weeks of training…" He continues unwavering.

"I know." I interrupt him before he can finish. "Call me crazy." I laugh nervously.

He can't help but ask the next obvious question. "How is it that you decided to run a marathon after only three weeks of training?"

He's going to think I'm crazy if I tell him the truth God. But You've opened the door for me to share what You're doing, so here goes…

"God put it on my heart to run this marathon." I profess with all the confidence I can muster.

The man looks at me strangely…almost like he can see right through me. My faith statement has now taken center stage in the middle of the two of us. The silence is heavy and seems to go on for an eternity as I await his reaction. I can't help but wonder if he too believes in God.

A big smile spreads slowly across the man's face accompanied by a twinkle in his eyes. Something warm begins to fill the space between us.

"Really?" He asks genuinely interested.

"Yes." I stand up straighter and don my fake courage. "I have no idea how it's going to go, but I know that, for some reason God, wants me to run this race. So here I am!" I gain confidence as I lay out my plan.

"I'm just going to start out and see what happens." I smile at him. "I look at it this way… I'm taking a journey…an adventure… I have no idea what I'll encounter, but I'm excited to see what God will do along the way. Maybe I won't get to the finish today. But maybe I will. I'm just excited to see what's going to happen."

The man gives me a long look sizing up my fortitude.

If I were him, I'd be questioning my sanity! I chuckle to myself.

"Mind if I run with you?" He asks in all seriousness.

"Really?" I laugh, certain he's joking. "I have no idea how fast I'll be able to run and I wouldn't want to hold you up."

It's hard to believe he actually wants to run with me.

"You won't hold me up," The man states without hesitation. "Let's give it a try! We can encourage each other along the way and you can tell me about your extensive training program."

The two of us laugh out loud together and his sense of humor isn't lost on me. Humor will probably come in handy today.

"Like I said, I have no idea how this is going to go for me," I smile hesitantly. "I'm not used to running with anybody. I always run alone. But if you're serious…I'm willing to give it a try." I give him one more chance to change his mind. "But if I'm going too slow, please don't think you need to hang back with me."

"It's settled then." The man's offer is genuine. "By the way, I'm Tom."

"I'm Renee, Tom." I announce realizing I'd been holding my breath in anticipation of his final decision. "Nice to meet you."

"Same here." He says as we shake hands.

I smile. It might be nice to have someone to run with today.

The race director interrupts our conversation and instructs everyone to move into place. The first wave of runners will start soon. Tom and I walk out into the street together. I'm not sure where I should place myself in this long line of elite runners. Tom suggests a starting position in the middle of the pack.

"You ready?" Tom asks as we listen for the signal that will start the race.

"Ready as I'll ever be." I laugh even more uncertain and unsure of what I've gotten myself into.

Lord, please help me. I know that it's You who led me here. You are the one that told me to run this race. I have no idea what is going to happen today but, I'm trusting You, God.

A Mother's Thoughts

I thought this was a good place for a pause in our story. Don't worry! You'll be able to read what happened in the next chapter. I just wanted to share a few things before we continue.

Depression and thoughts of suicide are a real battle. The pain is real. And suffocating. Depression is no laughing matter. I've had people in my life who don't understand how someone can be so "weak" as to resort to suicide.

My personal experience with depression was dark and painful. I hurt so bad. I just wanted the pain to end. I thought suicide might be my only means of escape from the unbearable pain I felt.

Satan seizes every opportunity to steal from us and destroy us. Satan is a liar and a thief. He wants to steal your life and destroy all God has planned for you. Depression is one of Satan's most evil tools. It's a full-fledged battle for one's soul. And thoughts of suicide are an assault on one's mind. Together, Depression and thoughts of suicide, combine to mount an attack to destroy us with a power that comes straight from the pit of hell.

There is a way out of the darkness. And it's not suicide. It's God.

God is near. Always. He promises never to leave us. When we cry out to God, He promises to hear us, listen to us and answer us. If we can take our focus off the darkness and turn toward the light, God will help us resist and overcome the temptations Satan puts in front of us.

A few things have helped me when depression threatens to overtake me. One is exercise. Taking walks. Running. Swimming. Anything that gets the heart pumping and the blood moving. Exercise is a known antidote for depression.

Another is changing my focus. Concentrating on the good in my life. Recognizing and appreciating what I have and focusing on the people in my life. Choosing to see the glass as half full, instead of half empty.

Setting goals that lead to experiencing a sense of accomplishment is another way to refocus. I start by creating a list of small goals I want to work to achieve and check them off as I accomplish them.

Telling someone how you feel and seeking help are also important tactics you can use to overcome depression. Telling someone not only exposes the secret, but telling someone a secret disarms it.

Secrets hold power the enemy can use against you. Satan loves to hide in the darkness of a secret and mount attacks from his evil hiding place. Telling someone forces your battle into the light and takes away the power a secret has over your life.

Take Aways

1. **God speaks in a still, small voice.**
   And after the earthquake there was a fire, but the LORD was not in the fire. And after the fire there was the sound of a gentle whisper. -1 Kings 19:12
2. **God speaks to us through thoughts that enter our minds.** But be careful to test every thought against

Scripture, because not every thought that enters our minds is from God. If a thought contradicts God's Word, it's not from God.

He who forms the mountains, who creates the wind, and who reveals his thoughts to mankind, who turns dawn to darkness, and treads on the heights of the earth— the LORD God Almighty is his name. - Amos 4:13

3. God has a plan for your life.
For I know the plans I have for you," declares the LORD, "plans to prosper you and not to harm you, plans to give you hope and a future. - Jeremiah 29:11

4. Nothing can separate us from God's love.
No, in all these things we are more than conquerors through him who loved us. For I am sure that neither death nor life, nor angels nor rulers, nor things present nor things to come, nor powers, nor height nor depth, nor anything else in all creation, will be able to separate us from the love of God in Christ Jesus our Lord.
- Romans 8:37-39 ESV

5. Satan comes to steal, kill and destroy. Jesus came to give us abundant life.
The thief comes only to steal and kill and destroy; I came that they may have life, and have it abundantly.
- John 10:10 ESV

6. When we are tempted, God will help us stand strong against temptation and provide a way out.
No temptation has overtaken you except what is common to mankind. And God is faithful; he will not let you be tempted beyond what you can bear. But when you are tempted, he will also provide a way out so that you can endure. - 1 Corinthians 10:13

Chapter 4

God Speaks Through His Word

For the word of God is alive and active. Sharper than any double-edged sword, it penetrates even to dividing soul and spirit, joints and marrow; it judges the thoughts and attitudes of the heart.
                                                                  - Hebrews 4:12

The Start

The long-awaited start is just moments away. But I'm unsure. Tom and I are probably a quarter mile from the starting line. I'm unsure if we'll be able to hear the loud electronic beep that starts the race? How will I know when we're…

And then it happens.

I now understand what the race director meant when he told us we'd start in waves. That's exactly what it feels like. A big wave. A wave that starts in the front of the pack, flows through Tom and I and surges through those behind us. The wave sweeps Tom and I up into an experience that is euphoric, powerful and exciting. Being carried along by the momentum of thousands of runners is an exhilarating feeling! I've never felt so light on my feet!

I'm really doing this! I say to myself finding it hard to believe the moment is finally here.

The mass of runners resembles that of a huge, dark speckled amoeba, crawling through the city, swallowing everything in its path. It's accompanied by the thunderous sound of thousands of footsteps hitting the pavement in an almost perfect rhythm.

It's close quarters running in the middle of the pack. Tom and I jockey for position as everyone tries to find enough personal space to run more comfortably. Some runners try to outrun the rest of us in an attempt to escape being jostled back and forth. I do my best to steer clear of the elbows around me.

Tripping and falling will not only be embarrassing, it would be downright dangerous.

Tom and I try to put some distance between ourselves and the largest mass of runners. We start running at a faster pace than I think I'll be able to manage. I really hope Tom's initial running pace isn't the pace he plans to run for the entire race. If that is the case, it won't be long before I lose my new running buddy.

I'm thankful when, after the first few miles, we break free of the pack and settle into a more manageable pace.

"You doing ok?" Tom breathes easily as we pass a group of five runners dressed so alike I assume they must all shop at the same clothing store.

"Doing good." I feel much more comfortable since Tom has chosen to slow down a bit. My breathing has relaxed and fallen into a much more manageable rhythm. And my heart doesn't feel like it's going to jump out of my chest.

Groups of runners, running at similar paces begin to form. As the race continues, there are times when Tom and I run up on groups up runners, and visit with them for a while, before moving on.

This is fun! The thought takes me by surprise. This is the first time in my life I've ever described running as fun and I know it's because of Tom. I know he's making all the difference today.

Thank you, God, for Tom. Thank you that he's with me today. I pray to myself. I can't believe I found someone at the starting line who is such a perfect match for me as a running partner. That is a miracle in and of itself!

For the first six miles, the running groups continue to space themselves out along the course. Then, at the end of Mile Five, the formation changes and the small groups of runners fall into a snakelike flowing river as we approach the entrance to the tunnel. The famous Detroit-Windsor Tunnel.

The *International Detroit Free Press Marathon* is one of the most unique marathons in the world. Runners start the race in Canada and finish the race in the United States. The route from one side of the border to the other takes runners through a mile long tunnel that lays on the bottom of the Detroit River, 75 feet under the river's surface. The tunnel is the start of Mile Six.

It takes a moment for our eyes to adjust when we enter the tunnel. The dim lamps cast dark shadows on the tunnel walls and the cold damp air sends a shiver through me. The sounds of heavy breathing and footsteps bounce off the cold cement and echo through the murky darkness. The dew on the ceiling forms small droplets that fall on us like a quiet misty rain as we pass through.

In the middle of the tunnel, Tom and I pass the Canadian and United States Flags painted side by side on the dewy tunnel wall. The two flags serve as a reminder that we are leaving one country and crossing over into the next. The thought of stopping and placing one foot on either side of the border crosses my mind. To be able to boast in the coming days that I was in two different countries at the same time would be fun and something few people can say they've done, but in the moment, while running through the tunnel, there is no time for that. Tom and I are making really good time and he'd most likely think I'd lost my mind if I stopped in the middle of the tunnel for such a stunt. And he'd probably run away from me as fast as he could!

I am in awe as Tom and I continue through the tunnel. To think we were literally running under the Detroit River is exhilarating.

I'm running the only marathon in the world where runners get to run underwater. I smile to myself...such a special marathon...*thank You, God.*

Mile 7

The tunnel expels Tom and I onto the streets of Downtown Detroit. The course then weaves its way up and down the city streets. Mile after mile Tom and I run, making new friends and trading stories as we push forward in our pursuit of the finish line.

Conversations between runners of all ages, shapes, sizes and ethnicities take place all around Tom and I. Getting to know people for the first time under such unnatural circumstances, is a unique and interesting experience. These are people from all over the world, that I will most likely never see again. And yet the bonds we form, during the miles we run together, have an eternal quality to them.

Topics of conversation during the day tend to center around running and training. And most everyone I meet eventually ends up asking me the same question, "How long have you been training?" As a result, I find myself continuously retelling my "lack of training" story. But every person I share my story with is excited for me. They encourage me and even motivate me with their belief that I'm going to be successful today. They seem to know that somehow, in some way, I'm going to finish this grueling race.

I'm thankful for the support of my new friends while certain our conversations are part of God's plan for each one of us. For some reason God wants those around me to hear my story and, in return, their positivity and encouragement strengthen my resolve and help propel me toward the finish line.

Mile 12

Tom is the first one to round the bend in the road as we approach Mile 12. I follow close on his heels. It's hard to believe we're near the half way point of the race.

"So, I'm curious." Tom waits for me to run up alongside him before continuing. "Why run a marathon after only three weeks of training?" His questions dives deep into my heart. "What's the back story?"

I hesitate to answer. I don't know if I want Tom to know the truth.

"If it's none of my business just tell me to take a hike." Tom laughs to help lighten the moment.

"Long story." I sigh out loud before proceeding cautiously. "God told me to run this race."

At first, Tom is silent. Then, after a few dozen more steps, he digs deeper. "Why?"

"It's a long story. But it comes down to the fact that I don't know if I want to live anymore." I watch for the coming judgement to shroud Tom's eyes.

"Wow...that's deep." Tom's kind, gentle spirit reaches out to my heart in comfort. "What makes you even ask yourself that question?"

"I don't know." I try to explain," Depression is a slippery slope. It can lead to a really dark place. Sometimes the pain of living outweighs the desire to live."

I'm not sure Tom understands so I continue. "Sometimes it just hurts too much to want to live anymore. You begin to think suicide is the only way to put an end to your pain. Suicide presents itself as the only answer."

A deep sadness flashes across Tom's face. "So how is this race part of that picture?" He runs closer to me in comfort, not wanting to miss what I'm about to say.

I understand Tom's confusion. It's hard for people to understand the darkness of depression unless they've lived with it.

"I'm not sure. I just know God told me to run this race. I don't know what will happen, but I have hope that God is going to do something in my life today…I'm trusting Him…. besides, I'm out of options." I pause hoping Tom can understand.

Tom absorbs the seriousness of our conversation in silence while spectators on both sides of the street yell out encouragement as we pass. After a few minutes of running quietly by my side, Tom turns to me. "Renee, I believe God is with you today. I can feel His presence." Tom's eyes burn hot with conviction. "I truly believe you're in the middle of a miracle."

The truth of Tom's statement is like a cool, refreshing river that sweeps into the deepest parts of my soul and floods the scorched and withered areas of my heart with life giving water. Something within me whispers that what Tom just said is true. It's hard to hold back my instant tears of gratefulness. Tom has no idea how badly I need a miracle. I turn to him and smile as a tear escapes, and softly flows down my face. Tom's eyes glisten and he nods in quiet acknowledgment of my joy. I'm too afraid to speak, for I know that if I speak, I'll end up sobbing. So I stay silent and turn my focus to the road ahead. Tom and I are halfway there. And the sound of our footsteps hitting the pavement together in unison, testifies to the bond God is creating between us.

Tom and I have been running at a comfortable pace for close to two hours. Thousands of spectators line the streets standing shoulder to shoulder in every direction. It's standing room only. Many applaud as we run past and shout out words of encouragement.

"Way to go!" "You can do it!" "Keep going!" "Great job!" And some along the route hold signs filled with various uplifting slogans.

Nearing the half way point of the race I spot Mike and Stacy standing on the side of the road shouting and waving.

"Is that your husband and brother?" Tom asks as I wave to the two of them.

"Yes." My huge smile is clear evidence of how important Mike and Stacy's presence is to me. It's wonderful seeing their familiar faces in the crowd, even if it's only for a short moment.

As Tom and I run up on the next water station, his smile tells me he understands how important my husband and brother's support is to me.

"Drink at every station." He cautions as I'm about to pass the water station without snagging a drink.

I quickly grab the small dixie cup the volunteer offers to me and dump the water down my throat without breaking stride. No matter if I'm thirsty or not, Tom's right. It's important to keep grabbing those little cups of water each time they're offered.

"Your body needs plenty of water in order to work well." Tom's been sharing tidbits of information like this with me all day. I'm thankful for his help as well as the distraction. Without the benefit of his knowledge, I'm not sure if I'd stand a chance of finishing this race.

Mile 14

Everything is going really well until Mile 14 when I zigzag in the road to avoid a small pothole and a sharp pain from just above my kneecap shoots up my left leg. I stifle a cry of pain and try to hide what's happening from Tom in hopes the pain will disappear. But just the opposite happens. With each additional step I take the pain becomes more constant and more painful.

Oh no…What am I going to do? The pain is getting

worse.

I can't run like this... Panic snakes its way into my heart.

I'm afraid to tell Tom. I don't want to worry him. But as a former athlete, I know the difference between good pain and bad pain. I know the difference between pain that's a result of being sore and pain that warns of pending injury. And the pain in my knee is bad. I know if I continue to run, I'll badly injure myself and eventually I'll be forced to pull out of the race altogether. I need help and I need it fast.

Fear propels me to reach out to the only One I know who can help me...

Lord, I know You want me to run this race...but I can't run like this. Please fix this pain in my knee.

Miraculously, within the next quarter mile, the pain completely disappears.

Mile 22

Going into Mile 22, I start to struggle with keeping up and maintaining our pace. I start feeling sick to my stomach. Something is wrong. My body feels like it's starting to shut down.

A debilitating wave of exhaustion slams into me and almost knocks me off my feet. I fight to continue running but I can't run away from reality. I'm not going to make it to the end.

I turn to Tom running alongside me. "Go ahead of me Tom." I don't want to hold him back.

Tom glances over at me, concern clouding his face. "No, it's ok. I'll stay with you."

"I'm holding you back." I don't want Tom to sacrifice his performance for me. "Go ahead." I repeat. I don't want to tell him I feel sick to my stomach.

"You aren't." Tom breaths out in frustration trying to convince me. "You aren't holding me back."

"Yes, I am," I argue. I know Tom has noticed a change in my pace. "I'll be fine. Go ahead of me. I'll see you at the finish line." I try to sound confident, but doubt is slowly starting to invade my thoughts.

I don't think I'm going to make it...

"Maybe we should just stop and walk a bit." Tom offers starting to realize something is really wrong.

"No, you go ahead. I'll stop and walk when I need to." I assure him best I can. "I'll be ok, I just need to slow down a bit and I don't want to hold you up." My breathing gets heavier.

"Tom...this morning...we talked about this...you need to go ahead." I struggle to get out my words as I implore him.

The look on Tom's face betrays him. And his eyes provide a window into his heart for me. A fierce battle has erupted inside of Tom. He's concerned...very concerned...but not for himself. He's worried about me.

Tom looks ahead and then back to me, struggling with his emotions as the battle rages within him. He doesn't know what to do...or what to say. He doesn't want to leave me.

My heart hurts knowing I'm the reason for the turmoil that's raging inside my new friend. I don't want to be the source of anything that causes Tom pain. The friendship he and I have built in these 22 short miles has become a bond that will connect us forever.

"Are you sure?" Tom says in anguish.

"Yes, I'm sure. Go ahead of me Tom. I'll be fine." I try again to sound convincing and strong.

The two of us continue to run. We only have four miles left. It's not much farther but I know I can no longer keep up with Tom. I continue to reassure him that I'll be ok.

After a little more bantering back and forth, I succeed in convincing Tom it's time for him to run ahead. He unwillingly concedes, lengthens his stride and begins to pull away from me.

I slow my pace so I can catch my breath.

Lord, thank You for Tom. I doubt if I'd have gotten this far without him. I say to myself, knowing it's the truth.

Tears fill my eyes. I'm so thankful for Tom but I can no longer match his pace. I don't have it in me any longer.

I watch as Tom puts more distance between the two of us. When he finally disappears from view a feeling of loneliness fills me. But I'm determined to finish this race even if I have to do it on my own. It's only a few more miles. It shouldn't take that much longer. I'll see Tom at the finish line.

Mile 24

My steps slow and falter and my feet stumble to a stop. I feel dizzy and disoriented. Black spots float through my vision and before I know what's happening, I throw up what little breakfast I had into the street.

Sick to my stomach I drop to my knees and sit on the hard cement curb with my feet together in the gutter. I wipe my mouth with my sleeve and use the back of my hand to clean off the dripping sweat from my forehead.

How can the last four miles be so much harder than the first 22? I rally my common sense to help me refocus.

I am so close…and yet…so far. I look up into the sunny, clear blue sky through fuzzy eyes and fight hard not to submit to another wave of nausea.

Lord…I need Your help…I can't do this.

My vision blurs. Everything is so hazy. Runners continue streaming past as I remain motionless on the curb. They are a defeating reminder of my inability to stand up, much less run.

I have to get up…I have to keep going. But how? I can barely move.

My brain starts playing tricks on me. Runners wrapped in foggy white clouds float past me. They appear angelic as they drift in and out of my vision and I fight the temptation to give into unconsciousness. Through the fog I spot a woman beckoning to me. Motioning upward with her arms. Urging me to stand. Her voice reaches me as an echo.

"Come onnnnnnn…you…can…do…it," she encourages through the cloudy white fog.

I look away and stare down into the gutter, my mind threatening to wander away in pursuit of an escape…a comfortable place where it can hide itself from my reality. I know I have to clear my head and get control of myself. But how?

All seems lost until Tom enters my thoughts.

I wonder if he's already at the finish line? I wonder smiling to myself thinking about our run together…and remembering Tom's kindness. I'm so thankful to have met

Tom…and I'm so thankful for his words about God being with us and his belief that I was in the middle of a miracle.

I can't quit now…Hope begins to rise within my heart. It's increasing brilliance starts clearing away the fog from my mind and something inside of me gives birth to a new strength that begins to fill me.

I place my hands on the curb determined to lift myself up. I use the curb to help stabilize my wobbly legs in an attempt to stand.

I just need to…get…up…and…put…one foot…in front… of the other…I tell myself determined to stand.

My arms work hard to help steady my teetering body. My legs groan under my full weight when I finally right myself. Once upright I struggle to maintain my balance.

I can do this…just…one…step…at…a…time…

A power not of this world lifts my right leg to take the first step. And in the next moment my left leg follows suit. One slow step after another returns me to the street to rejoin the race.

*I have to do this…even if I just walk the rest of the way…*I tell myself with renewed hope.

With each step forward my resolve increases.

*It's not much farther…*I reason with myself…*only a few more miles.*

Walking steps soon grow into slow jogging steps. And slow joggling steps, lead to small running steps. In the next quarter of a mile, I am running again and the finish is getting closer with each step I take.

I'm doing this! I'm going to finish!

Something inside tells me…it's true.

Mile 26

As I run over the final hill on Belle Isle, the finish line comes into view. I can't believe the end is now within reach.

There it is! I smile to myself in exhaustion hardly believing what I see up ahead.

I'm almost there! Adrenaline shoots through my body and sends my legs scampering down the last 20 yards of the home stretch toward the finish line. At the same time my spirit takes flight on wings of overwhelming joy and indescribable happiness.

A typhoon of emotions crashes into me as I cross the finish line. Elation. Unbelief. Happiness. Ecstasy. All flood into my heart in one glorious celebration.

I did it! 26.2 miles! I did it!

Raising my arms to the sky, I erupt into tears of unbridled joy. Unbelievable!

I did it! I can't believe it! I did it! I really did it!

Pure euphoria wraps me in its arms as the marathon workers cover my shoulders in an aluminum blanket and place a medal around my neck. Nothing in my life has ever come close to this mountain top experience and these feelings of accomplishment…thankfulness…victory…celebration…and humility.

The brightness of the moment sets fire to the darkness thats consumed my soul for months. The death grip the fingers of Depression have on my heart shatters in those moments of celebration and a divine peace is poured out into my soul.

Finally…after all these months, I have peace.

Crying tears of pure joy, I make my way through the finish gates. I scan the crowd, looking for the only three people I know. Mike, Stacy and Tom.

Thank you. God! Unbelievable! A miracle! I can't believe I just ran 26.2 miles.

Did that really just happen?! The moment is surreal.

Thank you, God! I know You ran with me today!

I can't stop crying happy tears as I make my way through the crowd looking for the guys. I did it. I finished the marathon.

A few minutes later I find Mike and Stacy waiting for me not far from the finish line. Their smiles and the look in Mike's eyes are the cherry on top of my life changing accomplishment.

Mike wraps me tightly in his arms.

"Congratulations!" His eyes glisten with unshed tears.

I try to find the words to tell Mike what I'm feeling. But I have no words to accurately describe my experience or the avalanche of emotions that continue to erupt within me. Today has been so much more than a race. Today has been a spiritual experience that was written into my life, by the Author of my life.

I feel like I'm walking on a cloud, three feet off the ground, soaring high above the earth on

Renee crosses the finish line of the Detroit Free Press International Marathon, Sunday, October 18, 1987.

blissful wings of pure elation. I'm so thankful for what God has done and how He used the marathon to shatter Depression's stranglehold on my life. Not only did God help me finish a 26.2-mile marathon, but He helped me grind Depression into the dust of my past.

I'm going to be ok. I'm certain of it.

Wiping happy tears from my face, I look for Tom. I told him I'd see him at the finish line but I haven't seen him yet. As I make my way through the crowd with Mike and Stacy, Tom is nowhere to be found.

"Ready to go home?" Mike grins and offers me his hand.

"Yes...." I turn my attention back to Mike and take his outstretched hand. "Yes…let's go home." I smile, so thankful he's with me.

As Stacy, Mike and I make our way to the parking lot to find the car and begin the two-hour journey home, a bit of sadness drifts into my heart. I didn't find Tom. I wanted to thank him. Another tear makes its way down my face as I get into the car and shut the door.

"Tom, wherever you are," I whisper to myself hoping God will somehow relay my message to my special friend, *"a million times thank you. I couldn't have done it without you."*

The Day After the Marathon

The next morning, I'm sitting at the counter in my bathrobe, sipping a cup of coffee and watching through my kitchen window as the sun rises over the lake in our back yard. The brightness of this new day seems more brilliant than ever before. A smile spreads across my face as I reflect on the events of yesterday.

God brought me to the starting line of my very first marathon. Then 26.2 miles later He carried me across the finish line. And in the end God used our journey through each mile to destroy Depression's hold on my life.

Wow! What a difference a day makes! The gift of divine peace from the day before still fills me.

Mike and I came home together last night and, for the first time in many months. the two of us spent the night under the same roof talking long into the night. We agreed to work on putting our marriage back together. We know we have a long road ahead of us, there is a lot to work through and there are many mountains to conquer, but we have chosen to conquer them together. And we will succeed. God will see to that.

The Sunday *Detroit Free Press Newspaper* is laying on the counter in front of me. Every runner, of every age, that ran in yesterday's marathon is listed in the paper, starting on the front page.

Earlier this morning I found my name in the women's age 25-29 results. It made me smile. I still can't believe I did it. I still can't believe I somehow accomplished the impossible. I know that it was only made possible, because of God's help. What happened to me yesterday was nothing short of a miracle…just as Tom predicted.

I turn to the paper to search the results for Tom's name. I

wasn't able to say goodbye yesterday but if I can find his name and get more information about him, then I can reach out and thank him for what he did for me yesterday.

During the race Tom told me he was 40 years old and from the Upper Peninsula. There weren't many runners in the marathon from the UP so that fact alone should help narrow down my search.

But as I search the results Tom's name is nowhere to be found.

That's strange…his name isn't listed in the men's 40 years old results…maybe I misunderstood him. Maybe he's listed in a different age bracket.

I increase my search to include all of the men's results but still no Tom. Never one to give up, I pour over the many columns of results numerous times knowing his name has to be listed somewhere but for some reason I'm just not seeing it.

No matter how carefully I search the newspaper looking for Tom's name, every unsuccessful review of the results, only leaves me more bewildered.

Why can't I find his name?

I keep going back to the paper certain that if I look just one more time, I'll find his name. But no matter how many times I look, my search comes up empty.

Why isn't his name here? Lord, I need to get in touch with him to thank him.

Not being able to find Tom's name leaves me feeling sad and empty inside. The newspaper results were my last hope to finding Tom to thank him.

Just as I'm about to search one last time, a Bible verse comes to mind.

"Don't forget to show hospitality to strangers, for some who have done this have entertained angels without realizing it."

I catch my breath.

Angels?

My eyes lift away from the newspaper to take in the beautiful skies of color outside my kitchen window as the truth reveals itself to my heart.

Had God sent an angel?!

That's crazy…and yet…

Could Tom have been an angel?

If Tom was an angel, that would explain why Tom's name isn't listed in the results.

Tears formed puddles in my eyes as certainty fills my heart.

Yes...I smile knowingly.

Maybe...just maybe...God had sent an angel.

A Mother's Thoughts

I believe God uses angels in our lives. I have too many stories of my own, and I've heard too many stories from others, to believe otherwise.

Running the *Detroit Free Press International Marathon* was one of God's greatest miracles in my life. God saw me in the darkness of depression and knew I was in serious peril. He knew what needed to be done to lift me out of the dark place I was in. He impressed upon me to enter the marathon, prepared me to run and sent Tom to run next to me.

Recently a friend pointed out something to me regarding what happened to me at Mile 22, the point at which Tom left me to finish the race on my own. That too was God's plan. For whatever reason, I needed to finish the race on my own. I had to do my part in order for God to complete His work in my life.

Suicide is never God's answer to pain or hardship or whatever struggle you might find yourself faced with. Satan will try to use suicide to destroy you and God's plan for your life.

But God has a much better plan for you.

If I ever question Gods existence or His love for me, I only need to think back to the miracle of the marathon. This memory always confirms for me the truth regarding who God is and how much He loves and cares for me. God feels the same way about you.

Run to God for shelter if you are battling an enemy that is threatening your life. God promises never to leave us or forsake us. He is as close as your next breath.

I'm thankful God impressed upon me to share the story of the marathon in this book. It's not easy retelling a painful story that makes me vulnerable to the judgement of others. It's not easy to admit such weakness. But if retelling this story can help others, who might be dealing with depression, intense pain or thoughts of suicide, then it's well worth taking the risk of sharing. I hope you find hope and comfort in what you have read.

Take Aways

1. **God speaks through His Word.**
   For the word of God is alive and active. Sharper than any double-edged sword, it penetrates even to dividing soul and spirit, joints and marrow; it judges the thoughts and attitudes of the heart. - Hebrews 4:12

2. **God is always with us. He will never, ever leave us.**
   Be strong and courageous. Do not be afraid or terrified because of them, for the LORD your God goes with you; he will never leave you nor forsake you. -Deuteronomy 31:6

3. **Whatever God calls us to do He will help us do.**
   I can do all things through him who strengthens me. - Philippians 4:13 ESV

4. **Sometimes God sends an angel.**
   Are not all angels ministering spirits sent to serve those who will inherit salvation? - Hebrews 1:14

Chapter 5

God Speaks Through Peace

Do not be anxious about anything, but in every situation, by prayer and petition, with thanksgiving, present your requests to God. And the peace of God, which transcends all understanding, will guard your hearts and your minds in Christ Jesus.

- Philippians 4:6-7

July 1995

Camping trips are one of our families most favorite things to do. It's something we look forward to all winter long as we brave the cold and freezing Michigan temperatures. Planning where we'll camp, and what we'll do once the weather breaks, helps get our family through each winter. When spring finally breaks and summer arrives, the four of us are eager to hit the road and visit all of our favorite camping spots. The last weekend of July in 1995 was no exception.

Friday capped off the end of a long work week. My husband Mike had gotten out of work early and I was starting week one of a two-week vacation. As a result, we were able to get an early start to the weekend. All week long we had been looking forward to two days of fun filled camping so when the time came, we were anxious to get on the road and put the work week behind us. The kids most of all. Once we started, it didn't take us long to pack up the motorhome and be on our way.

We arrived at the campground in plenty of time to set up camp, play some lawn games and eat dinner with our friends before it was time for the kids to hit the hay. After we finished putting the kids to bed, Mike decided to join them and turn in early. He'd had a long week.

I was still wide awake even though I hadn't slept much all week. So, I decided to mosey on down to the community campfire fully ablaze a few lots down from our campsite.

That weekend, most of the campsites in the campground were filled with our friends from church. We'd all signed up for the church camping trip back in May. Everyone was looking forward to spending a few days in the beautiful Northwoods of Michigan, and to top it off, the weatherman had promised a warm and sunny weekend. We had everything we needed for a perfect weekend.

Except for the storm raging in my soul.

I'd been struggling for months with indecision. No matter how many times I'd tried to put off making a choice, my dilemma always seemed to find its way back to the forefront of my mind. As a result, I'd been in an unsettled state of limbo for months.

Sometimes it's easier to make a decision, by not deciding. That is where I found myself on this beautiful summer weekend. Having chosen not to decide. Unfortunately, I'd found no peace in not deciding. And I'd also found there is no peace in being in limbo.

The decision I was trying to make would have been an easier one to make if it only affected me. But the fact that whatever I chose would have a huge impact on my husband and children…well that made my choice all the more important. I had to get it right. But I was struggling as to what "right" was.

At the time I was working two jobs from home. Most of my daytime hours were split between sewing dresses for my sewing business and coaching and managing the private age group swimming club I worked for. Every day I lived the same routine. In the late afternoon I'd make the fifteen-mile drive into town to attend swim practice where I'd spend three and a half hours coaching swimmers in the evening. Then after practice I'd return home to sit back down at the sewing machine and sew until one or two o'clock in the morning. I've been burning the candle at both ends while trying to raise two young children with my husband. The schedule I was keeping left little time for anything else. Even sleep.

I was exhausted. Something had to give.

The decision I had to make was if I should quit my full-time coaching job and concentrate solely on running my dress making business. The problem is, Mike and I weren't sure if we could afford to give up my coaching salary. We were a young family struggling to make ends meet and every nickel was important. How could I even consider quitting a job that provided us with half our household income?

And yet, I felt so unsettled. Something inside beckoned me to choose a different path.

Arriving at the campfire I took a seat on the log closest to the huge, roaring fire. There is nothing better than sitting under the stars next to a warm, crackling fire, on a warm summer night. The dancing flames possess a special hypnotizing magic all their own. The warmth of the fire felt good against my skin.

Usually, a campfire relaxed me. But not tonight. For weeks, nothing had been able to bring peace to my unsettled heart.

What's the right choice for our family? What's the best decision for our marriage?

I stared into the flames as my mind went back and forth trying to determine the best option.

I enjoyed being home with our two children during the day. But most of my time was spent jumping between the sewing machine, the computer and the telephone. As a result, I was often short and impatient with my children. How much of me was really available to them? At ages five and three they deserved so much more than I was able to give.

I let out a tired sigh and tried to find comfort in the warmth of the flames. Despite my troubles, the campfire was starting to calm my restless soul.

"Hi Renee! Mind if I sit here?" I looked up to find my friend Barb smiling at me and motioning to the seat next to me. Her warm brown eyes were the first to welcome us when we started coming to the church years ago.

"Hey Barb! Of course!" I smiled happy to share my log with her.

It had been a long time since I'd been able to visit with Barb. She was a woman I had always respected and admired.

Whenever Barb and I spent time together, I always walked away filled with so much of her shared wisdom. As a young mother, Barb has been an older woman I'd always looked up to.

"I think you have the best seat in the house!" Barb sat down and pointed to the basket sitting next to me. "Right next to the good stuff!"

I'd been too deep in thought to notice that the log I was sitting on was right next to the basket of smore making ingredients the campground staff had set out earlier in the evening.

"How've you been?" Barb asked as she settled in and grabbed a roasting stick and a marshmallow from the basket.

"Honestly?" I tried to read her face. How honest did she want me to be?

"Of course!" Barb's eyes met mine, full of warmth and concern.

"Troubled." I responded looking back into the fire.

"What's up?" She asked while putting the marshmallow on the end of her stick.

"I have a big decision to make." I paused a moment enjoying how the firelight was illuminating Barbs face before continuing. "I feel like God is telling me to quit coaching but I'm not sure. I want to do what He says, but I don't know how to be sure of what He wants. Barb, how do I figure out what God's will is for me and my family?

Barb pondered my question as she put the stick with the marshmallow into the fire. "Well...," she started, "when I'm trying to figure out God's will, there are three things I look for."

I couldn't wait to hear what Barb had to say. I wanted so badly to know how to determine God's will for my life...for my family's life.

"First," Barb began, "Is your decision in line with the principles of the Bible? Meaning, is what you are considering better for your marriage, your husband, your children...?

"God will never contradict His word." She continued as she pulled her marshmallow out of the fire to make sure it wasn't burning and then returned it to the fire. "If your choice goes against God's Word and His principles, then it's not God's will for your life."

"Ok...that makes sense." I picked up a stick near my feet and began poking the fire. "What's the second one?"

"Are doors opening in that direction?" Barb grabbed two graham crackers and a square of chocolate from the basket.

"And other doors shutting?" I asked as something stirred in my heart.

"Yes." She confirmed and took the now golden-brown roasted marshmallow out of the fire. "Sometimes God directs us using circumstances. Some people call it coincidence. But I don't believe there are any coincidences in life. God is in charge of everything in the universe and He will use circumstances to guide us by opening and shutting doors in our lives. I often pray for Him to do just that...open and shut doors!" She grinned and looked up into the sky as though talking to God. "Please God! Only open ONE door! Only open the one door You want me to walk through!" Barb turned to me, her face beaming. "It's a lot easier that way...only having one door to choose from!"

I smiled as I basked in the warmth of Barb's wisdom. How simple she made it all sound.

"Also, once a door is shut, it's important not to try to kick it back open." Barb grew more serious. "Sometimes we tend to do that...try to kick the door back open after God has shut it" She smiled as she placed the warm marshmallow on one of the two crackers.

Our talk was giving me hope that maybe I really could figure out God's will for my life.

"Ok...what's number three? Having a checklist, I could work through, would certainly help in determining God's will for my life.

"You will have God's peace about your decision. The kind of peace that surpasses all understanding. There may be no logical or rational reason for the choice you've made. And to the world your choice might even seem a little bit crazy or unrealistic. But the deep peace that comes and fills you, will confirm to you, that you know...because you know...because you know...that it's the right choice for you," Barb concluded confidently.

I thought about what Barb said for a while as she added a square of chocolate on top of the marshmallow, topped it with the second of the two crackers and squeezed the sweet concoction together to make a smore sandwich.

"Wow...I've never heard any of this before Barb." I paused still considering her words. "Thank you...thank you for sharing with me! I'm going to find time tomorrow to talk to Mike about what you've shared and see what he thinks." I couldn't believe how simple and easy Barb made it sound.

"Want one?" Barb asked offering me her smore.

"No thanks." I replied looking into the crackling fire deep in thought. "I need to lose a few pounds."

"Don't we all!" Barb laughed, standing up to leave, smore in hand." I guess that's my cue to find my husband, and unburden myself of these calories!"

"Thank you again, Barb," I continued gazing into the flames. "I can't begin to tell you how helpful you've been."

"Glad to be of help." Barb started to leave, then hesitated and turned back toward me. "And Renee...you know you can always give me a call if you ever need to talk."

I turned my gaze from the fire. to Barb's caring eyes and smiled. "I know...thanks Barb...I really appreciate you taking the time to share with me."

A lump formed in my throat as Barb turned and walked away. Her concern meant so much to me. She'd helped more than she realized. She had certainly given me a lot to think about.

After Barb left, I sat by the fire thinking long into the night. I'd find a moment to talk to Mike tomorrow. Together we'd talk through the three points Barb had shared. And together we'd make a decision about what we should do.

***

The next afternoon, Mike and I talked through the three points Barb had shared with me the night before. The two of us agreed that it seemed like God was telling me to quit coaching. But the thought of quitting coaching was a scary step to take. Mike and I didn't see how we could survive on half our household income. The safe choice would be to wait until December to make a final decision. Because in December we'd have more information and we'd also have the final end of the year sales numbers from my business. So, after spending a few hours going through all the pros and cons of each option, Mike and I ultimately agreed that waiting until December, to make our final decision, would be our best choice.

But something about our decision to wait until December didn't sit right with me. It was reasonable to wait, but I was still unsettled. I still wasn't at peace. Something inside me didn't want to wait until December. I wanted to decide NOW. And I knew what I thought the decision should be.

The weekend quickly passed and with the dawn of Sunday morning came the sad realization it was time for us to pack up and return home. That morning, before the kids and Mike got out of bed, I went for a run hoping to find the inner peace that was still alluding me.

Running down the road away from the campground, I couldn't help but think about the decision Mike and I had made the day before. The more I thought about it and the farther I ran, the more upset I became.

If it was the right decision, then why didn't I feel the peace Barb spoke of?

Waiting until December is the safe thing to do. I argued with myself. *It's the reasonable choice and it makes sense...*

But I don't want to wait until December. Myself argued back. *I want to decide NOW*! And I'm pretty certain I know what we should do.

But I'm afraid. A small voice inside confessed.

I stopped running in the middle of the road.

I couldn't take another step. I was crying too hard to breathe, much less run. The fear I felt was paralyzing. I didn't want to be afraid. But I was.

My words to God gushed out in gut wrenching sobs.

"Lord...I need...to know...without a doubt...what You...want me to do." I sobbed as I walked along the road. "Please...show me...what...You want...me to do."

Little did I know then, but in three days' time God would not only show me, but He'd shake apart my world.

August 2, 1995

Three days later, after we got home from the camping trip, I was busy in the house getting ready for our daughter Lindsey's third birthday party. Mike was in town picking the kids up from day camp. They would be home any minute along with our family and friends who were joining us for the birthday celebration. And I was only half way through my "to do" list for the party.

In the middle of my putting the food out on the back deck patio table the phone rang. I hurried inside to grab the phone and the birthday cake at the same time.

"Hello?" I answered cradling the phone on my left shoulder as I tried to balance the cake and maneuver myself through the swinging back door.

"Hello Renee, this is Gary." Gary was the president of the board of directors for the swimming club I worked for.

"Hi Gary." I uttered in greeting wondering why he was calling me while the swimmers were on break and I was on vacation. I had no idea my entire world was about to come crashing down all around me.

"Renee your coaching services will no longer be needed." Gary announced nonchalantly.

My jaw dropped and my mind snapped shut. The physical jolt sending shock waves across my body caused the birthday cake to teeter in my hand. Before the cake face planted itself onto the back deck, I stabilized myself and got the cake safely to the patio table.

I must have misunderstood. I reasoned absent-mindedly setting the cake down. Looking out over the back yard into the horizon of a brilliant blue sky, Gary's seven words exploded in my heart...*your coaching services are no longer needed...*

He's firing me? My mind struggled to accept my new reality. *I was being fired?*

Gary was still talking on the phone but I could no longer hear what he was saying. I tried to focus on his words, but my mind refused. After a few moments Gary thanked me for my service and abruptly ended the call without giving me a reason for why I was being terminated.

I hung up the phone and picked my mouth up off the floor, stunned. Fourteen years of dedication and commitment had just been carelessly tossed aside in a quick two-minute phone call. I caught my breath as a mixture of emotions swallowed me.

Did that just happen? I was confused, bewildered and shocked. But half of me was also happy, excited and relieved. A huge burden had suddenly fallen off my shoulders and for the first time in a long time, I felt peace...a peace that surpassed all understanding...the peace Barb spoke about.

But the peace was short lived when, within minutes, pride rose up to take a stand in my heart.

"He can't do this! The parents support me! I'll call them. I'll start making phone calls tonight! I'll fight this!" I started to dig in my heels and put together a battle plan.

But the peace returned and used a truth that rose up from deep within me to push aside the pride in my heart.

This was from God.

Three days earlier, I'd prayed and asked God to tell me what to do. I'd asked Him to show me without a doubt what HE wanted me to do. Gary's phone call was God's answer. The phone call was God showing me what to do. God was the One who had slammed the door shut. Not Gary. God had intervened and answered my cry just as I'd asked Him to. And now I had to choose.

Was I going to trust God? Or was I going to try and kick the door back open?

***

Mike and the kids got home just as I finished setting up for the party. When they walked through the door, I told Mike about the phone call. To my surprise he was elated. In fact, they all were...my husband AND my two children.

"Sew Mommy, sew!" The kids started chanting and dancing. "Sew Mommy, sew!"

I wasn't sure if they were just trying to make me feel better, but the picture of my children dancing around the table, accompanied by my smiling husband beating a spoon on a frying pan, made me laugh uncontrollably.

In the middle of the ruckus my in-laws opened the front door with arms overflowing in birthday gifts. The kids spotted their grandparents first and ran to the door to tell them what had just happened to me. Mike's parents' response surprised me. They were happy I'd lost my job. In a room full of smiles, my in-laws encouraged me to put all my time and effort into my business and our family and not worry about the rest. Their support sealed the deal and confirmed for me that God had indeed answered my prayer.

***

As word spread throughout the parents on the swim team the phone started ringing. Team parents called day and night to express their concern over what had happened and offer their support. Team board members called to tell me they were as surprised as I was. They assured me they had never discussed, or approved, plans to end my employment. They shared their plan to call a meeting to reverse the decision and send the board president packing.

As flattered as I was by their support, I knew what I had to do.

"Thank you for calling." I repeated to each caller. "I appreciate your support. But I believe this is an answer to something I prayed about last weekend."

I then shared with each caller how I'd asked God to tell me, without a doubt, what He wanted me to do. And how I knew, without a doubt, that leaving coaching was the right choice…for me, for my family and for my marriage. Even if it made no logical sense to anyone else.

By the end of the week, I finally understood what Barb had tried to explain to me the night we sat together at the campfire. Because the peace Barb spoke of that night, was now finally mine.

April 1996

"Do you have your cleats?" I turned to ask my son Michael, who was sitting in the back seat behind my husband.

"Yes mom," he answered looking up from playing his

hand-held video game.

I turned back around and looked anxiously out the front window of the van checking our progress. We were heading down Saginaw Rd in Midland to the baseball field. The game would start in 30 minutes. Michael's coach didn't like it when his players were late. Taking into consideration the school zone and reduced speed limit ahead, I figured we'd still make it to the field in time for warmup. That is until the traffic light in front of us chose not to cooperate with my travel plan.

I let out a heavy, impatient sigh as Mike slowly came to a stop at the red light in front of the driveway leading into high school parking lot.

We should still make it in time. I assured myself, annoyed at the red light.

I put my left elbow on the armrest and, with my chin in hand, looked straight ahead. My fingers began using my knee as a drum as I patiently waited for the light to change and begged the red light to reconsider its current choice of color.

How long was it going to take the light to turn green? Unfortunately, patience wasn't something I'd ever mastered.

As I considered how the coach might react if Michael was late, something outside my window drew my attention to the high school parking lot and my fingers stopped drumming. The lot was filled with cars. And the fact that I knew who owned each and every car parked in the parking lot was not lost on me.

They're having swim practice. My thoughts whispered to me. *The swim team is in the pool right now. I haven't thought about swim practice in almost a year.* As the thoughts flowed into my mind, something became abundantly clear.

This is exactly where I was a year ago.

I smiled into the window feeling like I do when I watch the dawning of a new and glorious day.

But I wasn't there today...today I was on my way to my son's baseball game.

The tears trickled down my face and were caught in my reflection in the window. I smiled and turned to Mike sitting in the driver's seat.

"Think of all I would have missed." I admitted as the truth of what had been flowed through me.

Mike glanced at the parking lot, and gave me a knowing smile as the light turned green.

Thank you, God. I whispered as Mike picked up speed and headed toward the baseball field.

A Mother's Thoughts

I never regretted my decision to quit coaching. My family and I were all so much happier for the change. As the year of that decision drew to a close, we experienced no change in our lifestyle. Logically it made no sense. How could a family of four lose half their household income and experience no change? I didn't have an answer then and I don't have an answer now. God's plans have never made sense to me. But for some reason, they always seem to work out so much better than any plan I ever come up with.

After firing me, Gary somehow became one of my biggest supporters. When a child needed help with swimming strokes, Gary would tell the parents I was the best in the business and he'd refer them to me for help. Many years later after I was fired, Gary and I would join forces and coach a high school team together. How that happened is a story all its own, but the two of us had a wonderful time coaching together for almost a decade, and we had some of the most successful high school swimming teams in the state.

Gary would also become my friend. It's hard to imagine how God can take a person one considers an enemy, and turn him into a friend. But somehow God is able to do things like that. It just goes to show you that God can truly do anything and He is absolutely in control of everything. My new friendship with Gary was a reminder that God has quite a sense of humor and that I should never say "never" when it comes to God!

The year Gary fired me, my sewing business experienced record sales. At the end of that year, Mike and I had more money in the bank than we'd ever had in the bank while I was coaching. God provided for us in ways I never could have imagined.

As the years passed, God continued to teach me about the importance of keeping His order for my life. The order of God first, my husband second and our family third. God taught me that the rest of the things in life must always come behind those first three priorities. He also gave me real-life experiences to practice what He'd taught me like the day I was getting ready for yet another craft show.

That afternoon I had a three-foot-high mountain of fabric pieces sitting on the floor next to me and my sewing machine. The show I was preparing for was the coming weekend which meant I only had three days to finish sewing the pile. Getting through the pile was going to take either a small miracle or round the clock sewing.

But my son had a baseball game in a few hours. So, I was now faced with a choice. I could either stay home and finish the pile, or I could leave the pile and go to my son's baseball game.

I'd been in similar situations before and over the years I'd learned my lesson.

"God, I can either miss Michael's baseball game or finish this pile. I know that Your order for my life is family first before work. So, I'll tell You what…," I bartered. "I'm going to go to the baseball game this afternoon and let You determine what happens to this pile."

I smiled knowing I'd made the right choice.

It wasn't the first time, nor the last, that I'd go to a family event and trust God with what to do with a pile of cut fabric. Sometimes God enabled me to finish the pile before the weekend, and sometimes He didn't. But, in the end, whatever He did always fit the need and was the best for me and my family.

Over the years I've added to Barbs wise list of three. The additions I've made to her list, have also helped me to determine God's will for my life. Having said this, I do have one caution! **None of the following guidelines should ever be used as standalone guideline in determining God's will for your life.** Whenever possible, you should seek confirmation of God's will through multiple ways. And keep in mind that anything that contradicts God's Word, the Bible, is NOT God's will for your life. Because God will never contradict His Word.

How to Determine God's Will for Your Life

1) **Seek Godly council.**
   Seek the council of godly people you trust, who can help you sort through the puzzle pieces of your choices. Do not seek counsel from the ungodly. Look to seasoned saints who walk closely with the Lord. What you choose today will determine your tomorrows.

2) **Pay attention to what those who love you most are saying.**
   Especially if they are all saying the same thing. God often uses our loved ones to guide us.

3) **A house divided against itself cannot stand.**
   Our spouse is one of the primary people God uses to speak to us and guide us. God often guides me through my husband. If my husband is not in agreement with the choice I'm about to make then, for me, it's a big STOP SIGN from God. Maybe God is saying "no". Or maybe God is saying "wait". But there is one thing for certain, I am not to move in any direction until my husband and I are on the same page. And that means not badgering my husband to get him on my same page. If my husband doesn't get on my same page on his own, then most likely God is telling me "no" and I need to accept that answer.

4) **Don't make a decision based solely on money.**
   Either the lack of, or the abundance of. If money is sitting on one side of the scale and everything else involved in the choice is sitting on the other, do not make a choice based solely on money.

5) **Don't make a decision based on fear.**
   Confusion brings fear. And God does not give us a spirit of fear. Satan is the author or confusion and fear. As Barb shared with me sitting beside the campfire, if what we are about to choose is God's will for our life, we will have peace. 2 Timothy 1:7 states *For God has not given us a spirit of fear, but of power and of love and of a sound mind.*

6) **Don't make a decision based on false guilt.**
   Learn the difference between real guilt and false guilt. Satan will use the latter to draw you away from God's will for your life.

7) **Keep God's order for your life and make decisions accordingly.**
   God is first, your marriage is second, and your family is third. Everything else falls below the top three. Life can get really messy, really fast and we can completely veer off the road of God's will for our life when we don't keep the order He's given us to live by.

8) **Prayer and fasting are two powerful tools God gives us to use.**
   Consider both prayer and fasting when you have a hard decision to make or you are desperate for God to intervene in your life or the lives of others. I believe that something extraordinary happens in the spirit world when we fast and pray. Especially when we fast and pray in love. I've had countless experiences when impossible strongholds have been shattered when I've obeyed God's call to fast and pray.

Take Aways

1. **God speaks through peace.** God's Holy Spirit gives us peace. We will not feel peace outside of God's will.
   Do not be anxious about anything, but in every situation, by prayer and petition, with thanksgiving, present your requests to God. And the peace of God, which transcends all understanding, will guard your hearts and your minds in Christ Jesus. - Philippians 4:6-7

   For God is not the author of confusion, but of peace, as in all the churches of the saints. - 1 Corinthians 14:33 NKJV

2. **God speaks through godly council.**
   Listen to counsel and receive instruction, That you may be wise in your latter days. There are many plans in a man's heart, Nevertheless the Lord's counsel—that will stand.
   - Proverbs 19:20-21 NKJV

3. **God speaks through prayer.**
   And this is the confidence that we have toward him, that if we ask anything according to his will, he hears us.
   - 1 John 5:14 ESV

4. **God responds when we pray.**
   But you, Lord, are a shield around me, my glory, the One who lifts my head high. call out to the Lord, and he answers me from his holy mountain.   - Psalm 3:3-4

5. **God is a God of order.**
   For God is not a God of disorder but of peace.
   - 1 Corinthians 14:33

Chapter 6

God Speaks Through Dreams

For God speaks again and again, though people do not recognize it. He speaks in dreams, in visions of the night, when deep sleep falls on people as they lie in their beds. He whispers in their ears and terrifies them with warnings. He makes them turn from doing wrong; he keeps them from pride.

— Job 33:14-17 NLT

February 1988

I'm jolted awake in the middle of the night with a strong sense of urgency to act. My heart is racing and I'm uncomfortably hot. Wiping the sweat from my forehead I throw off the covers.

I have to call my brother.

But it's 1:00 a.m.!

But the dream...it was so real. I have to make sure he's ok.

Turning on the bedside table lamp, I pick up the phone and dial my brother's number in Michigan. One ring, two rings, three rings...

Come on...pick up...

The phone continues to ring. My brother is not picking up. But the urgency in my heart won't subside.

I have to reach him.

I dial his number again. One ring, two rings...still no answer. My heart pounds faster.

I try his number a third time. One ring, two rings...still no answer.

Why isn't he answering? I'm desperate. *Who can I call to go check on him to make sure he's ok? ...Mom!*

I dial my mom's number.

"Hello." Her sleepy voice answers.

"Mom?" I'm so relieved she's picked up.

"Renee?" Concern fills her voice. All moms know a middle of the night phone call is never a good thing.

"Mom," my voice starts to tremble, "I had a dream...a dream about Stan. I tried to call him but he's not answering. Can you try to get a hold of him?"

"Renee what's going on?" Mom's voice is strong. She's wide awake.

"I'm in Wisconsin. Staying overnight at a hotel. I got here yesterday. I have a swim meet this weekend." I hurry to explain.

"I just had a dream. I dreamt I called Stan on the phone but someone else answers. In my dream I can see Stan drowning in the bathtub because he's overdosing on drugs. But I can't get the person on the phone to go to him. No matter what I say, the person won't go check on Stan. I keep telling the person to get Stan. All the while I can see Stan drowning in the bathtub but I can't get to Stan to save him. Mom, I have a bad feeling. I've got to reach Stan. Can you call him?"

"Ok, I'll call him and see if he'll pick up." Mom knows of the ominous dreams I've had in the past. Dreams that have strangely lined up with real life events.

"Mom, if Stan doesn't pick up, you have to go to his house." I implore her before she hangs up. "You have to make sure he's ok!" I can't shake the feeling I have.

"Ok, but let me call him first and see if he'll pick up." I can hear Mom getting out of bed. I'm thankful she's taking me seriously.

"Ok, please call me back and let me know what you find out." I'm thankful for Mom's help but I'm still concerned and anxious something could be wrong with my brother.

"I will." Mom replies and hangs up first.

I slowly put the phone receiver back on the hook.

What if she can't get a hold of him? What will she find if she goes over to his house to check on him?

Oh my gosh! It's the middle of the night! Doubt begins to creep into my mind. *It's almost two in the morning! Maybe the dream is all about nothing. Maybe it's just my imagination running wild. But why did I have the dream? And why did it seem so real?*

Stan's not using drugs. He's been clean for over a year. He's probably sleeping and that's why he's not answering the phone.

Stan has a 14-month-old son who doesn't yet sleep through the night. A good night's sleep is hard for him to come by these days. And here I am, waking him in the middle of the night, because of a dream!

But my sense of urgency won't go away. I have to make sure my brother is ok even if it means waking him up in the middle of the night.

Lord, please keep my brother safe. I have no idea why this is happening or why I feel like I do. Maybe I'm crazy, but I can't shake this feeling. I have to make sure my brother's ok. Lord, please help my mom get a hold of him. Don't let her stop until she does. And please have him be ok.

I get out of bed and begin pacing back and forth across my hotel room praying…praying for the phone to ring…praying for my brother to be ok…praying for God to intercede in whatever is happening…

Fifteen minutes passes, then 30…I continue to pace and pray.

Please God. Let my brother be ok. Help my mom reach him. I repeat over and over.

15 minutes passes…then 30…then 45 minutes…and then finally… the ringing of the phone shatters the unbearable silence.

My feet dart across the hotel room floor and I grab the phone before it rings a second time.

"Hello?" I answer, in anticipation, hoping it's mom.

"I heard you had a bad dream."

My knees collapse and I crumble into a pile on the floor at the sound of my brother's voice. My chin drops to my chest in relief as the dam inside my heart bursts open and tears flow freely down my face.

"Are you ok?" I ask my brother choking down a sob.

"I'm fine…I'm ok." Stan sounds sleepy. "Tell me about

your dream."

"I'm so sorry to wake you." I apologize feeling bad I've made such a big deal of a dream. "It's probably nothing...but I had to call to make sure you were ok."

"It's ok...tell me about your dream." My brother repeats, not at all upset with me,

In the next few minutes, I proceed to tell Stan about my dream. And then as I finish, before I can even think about what I'm about to say...the words tumble out on their own...

"Stan you have to get off the drugs."

Until tonight everyone in our family has been under the impression Stan had stopped using drugs. That he had been clean for almost 18 months. There was no evidence to the contrary. But tonight...somehow...or maybe Someone...has revealed the truth to me.

"Is this the kind of life you want for your son?" I ask confronting my brother knowing how much he loves his son.

Stan doesn't deny, or admit, to using drugs. He doesn't even get upset with me for insinuating he's using drugs. The two of us spend the next hour talking on the phone. We talk about how much my brother loves his little boy and the kind of life he wants for his son. We talk about the Lord and faith and about God's love. That middle of the night phone call ends up being one of the best conversations I've ever had with my brother.

In the wee hours of the morning, when Stan and I finally say goodnight, I hang up the phone thankful my brother's ok, but puzzled. I can't help but wonder why it all happened...the dream...the phone call...the conversation...why?

Getting back into bed, I settled in under the covers and turned off the light. Staring up at the dark ceiling I continued to wonder "why". Why did God give me a dream, wake me up in the middle of the night and fill me with panic and a strong sense of urgency to call my brother?

Why God?

We did cover a lot of ground in our conversation. Maybe tonight just happened to be the night when Stan's heart was open to listen to something I said in our conversation?

Yes, that's probably it...

God always knows the time and place when a person's

heart is open to hearing and listening to something God wants a person to hear.

Yes, that's probably it...that's probably what tonight was about...

Even though I have no idea what I might have said, that God may have wanted Stan to hear, I accept the possibility it might be true and it may be what tonight was all about. Feeling sleepy, I stretch out on my side, fluff up my pillow and close my eyes.

Thank you, Lord, for tonight. Thank you for the wonderful conversation I had with Stan. Thank you for whatever tonight was about. And thank You for loving my brother and for always protecting him. \

Spring 1988

As the months pass by, the night of the dream begins to dim until it is all but forgotten. In the spring of 1988, Stan is arrested for possession of narcotics, convicted and sentenced to a year in jail. After he's incarcerated, letters and occasional phone calls are the only means of communication I have with my brother.

God brings my brother to my mind constantly and, as a result I pray for Stan day and night while he's in jail. Not a day goes by when I don't think about my brother and wonder how he's doing. I miss him, but I know that somehow God is working in his life behind bars.

A few months into his sentence, Stan rededicates his life to Christ. He shares this with me during a phone call one day. I'm so happy for him. His decision to recommit his life brings me to tears and gives me hope that life will be different for him and his family once he's released from jail.

The months crawl slowly past while we wait out Stan's incarceration. As the days of summer begin to shorten and the leaves start changing color, there is talk of Stan getting an early release in November. Although this is wonderful news, I ask God to keep Stan in jail until his faith is strong enough to withstand the temptations of his past life.

Stan and I continued to talk on the phone while we waited

for a decision regarding his upcoming release. Our conversations are full of hope for a different life and a bright future for him and his family. Stan often talks about all the things he wants to do for God when he's finally released.

Then in November, we get the news.

Stan will indeed be released early. Two days before he gets out of jail, my brother calls me one last time.

"Renee, I feel so good!" Stan can't wait to get back home. "I'm so thankful to God! I've been reading my Bible every day and I can't wait to get out and live my life for Him."

Stan and I talk about all the changes God has made in Stan's heart and in his life. And how incredible it is that God has rescued Stan from such a hopeless, dark life.

Over the past few months, as Stan has shared bits and pieces of his life with me, I can clearly see the miracle God has performed in my brother's life. And I keep thinking his amazing story of redemption needed to be shared.

"Stan, your story is so powerful. It's a miracle you're even alive. Your story is such a wonderful testimony to what God can do in a person's life. It could probably help so many people. You really need to write your story down so it can be used to help others." I know Stan has beat the odds and is still alive, but only by the grace of God.

"I will tell my story someday...," Stan's smile finds its way to me through the phone lines, "...and I know just the right person to write it." My brother knows how much I love to write.

"I would love to do that!" I can't believe my brother really wants me to write his story. "

I can't wait to hear more.

"Are there other things you can tell me...things you've lived through?" My mind starts formulating a plan to start writing my brother's story.

"I really can't go into it right now over the phone," Stan answers. Although I'm unaware, my brother is fully aware of the fact that people listen in on phone conversations prisoners make from jail. "But I'll tell you one thing. Do you remember the time you called me in the middle of the night? You were ..."

"Yes! I was in Wisconsin...at a swim meet!" I interrupt my brother's explanation. "I had a dream...and I called you because I was worried about you."

"Yup, that's it." My brother responds remembering the details of that evening last winter. "Do you know what I was doing that night just before you called?"

"I have no idea." I reply confused, my curiosity piqued by my brother's question.

I'd closed the chapter of that night. I assumed God had reached out to Stan in the middle of that particular night because it was the moment Stan's heart was open to listening to whatever God wanted to say to Stan that night. Stan now had my full attention as he continued.

"That night I was freebasing."

My brother's confession puts me in a choke hold that makes my breathing stop and makes my heart skip several beats. My eyes grow wide as saucers as I'm confronted with the truth.

He was freebasing? Cocaine?

"I was about to take another hit when I got mom's call." Stans voice grows soft. "She told me you had a dream and I needed to call you…" His voice trembles. "After I talked to you that night, I couldn't do it…after we hung up I put the drugs away."

Stunned silence left the two of us listening to the static sound of the telephone line. My brother broke the silence first.

"I've often wondered if I'd be alive today had you not called me that night," he professed to me in a whisper.

Through the phone lines I hear my brother's tears join mine. I had no idea what he was doing the night I called and told him about my dream. I only knew I'd a bad dream. And God had impressed upon me a strong sense of urgency to call my brother to make sure he was ok.

A Mother's Thoughts

I believe God uses many ways to call on us to intercede for others. Sometimes He impresses upon us to pray. Sometimes He impresses upon us to turn the car around and go to a person's home. And sometimes He gives us a dream that causes us to act.

I believe God can, and does, speak to us through dreams. I have no doubt God saved my brother's life on that cold winter night, in Michigan, in February of 1988. The greatness of a God who will reach across hundreds of miles to intervene and save the life of someone I love leaves me in awe. I will always be thankful God intervened to save my brother's live using a dream and a phone call.

In 2003 Stan took a powerful stand in his life and swore off all drugs and alcohol. In 2023 he celebrated 20 years of sobriety. My brother's life is such a wonderful God story! I still hold out hope that, someday, he will share his life story with others. And I still believe his story can be used to change lives.

Take Aways

1. **God speaks through dreams.**
   For God speaks again and again, though people do not recognize it. He speaks in dreams, in visions of the night, when deep sleep falls on people as they lie in their beds. He whispers in their ears and terrifies them with warnings. He makes them turn from doing wrong; he keeps them from pride. - Job 33:14-17 NLT

2. **God is always watching over us and those we love. Thankfully, God never sleeps.**
   The Lord keeps you from all harm and watches over your life. The Lord keeps watch over you as you come and go, both now and forever. - Psalm 121:7-8 NLT

3. **Prayer is a powerful tool. It connects us to God's power through the Holy Spirit.**
   The prayer of a righteous man is powerful and effective.
   - James 5:16

Chapter 7

God Speaks Through Unanswered Prayer

Do not be anxious about anything, but in every situation, by prayer and petition, with thanksgiving, present your requests to God. And the peace of God, which transcends all understanding, will guard your hearts and your minds in Christ Jesus. - Philippians 4:6-7

October 1997

She is dying. Six months ago, she was diagnosed with 33 tumors on her liver and given four to six months to live. It's now October…the dawn of month number six.

In July, Mom got all her affairs in order and started planning for her death. All the while continuing to hope for a miracle. Any miracle that would either defer or cancel her death sentence would suffice. Anything.

A few months ago, Mom came to me and asked permission to die in our home. Her request took my breath away. Of course, I said "yes". I wouldn't want anything less for my mother. Whatever I can do to bring her comfort. Whatever I can do to help her. I want to be there for her…for whatever she needs…from now until the end.

This month Mom moved into our house. It's been hard having her live with us. The history I have with my mom has created a lot stress and challenges for all of us. There is a lot of baggage my mom and I carry with one another. Really heavy baggage. As a result, the skeletons from our past surface daily. But I have to sort out and battle through the closet of skeletons on my own. My mom only has enough energy to fight one battle. The battle for her life.

Often times I escape to the basement to cry. I sob all types of tears. There is so much grief to work through. Not only do I grieve the imminent loss of my mother, but I grieve the end of the mother-daughter relationship I always wanted, but we never had.

A relationship I always held out hope for. A relationship that doesn't have a chance now because cancer has taken all hope away. Every day, in the bowels of our basement, I grieve what could or should have been.

And I feel angry.

Angry our relationship isn't better. Angry I have no answers. Angry I have nothing to offer her. Angry I have no good choice to make in this situation because…my mother is dying. And I don't have the power to stop death.

Most every day Mom and I have deep conversations about faith and trusting God. Most of our conversations consist of me watching silently, from some corner of the room, while mom fights with God. In those moments I can't help but wonder if my mom is trying to convince God. Maybe she's hoping He'll change His mind about ending her life.

Mom spends her days searching the internet for a possible cure and attending healing services at different churches. She also spends a lot of time responding to all kinds of advertisements from quacks who hold out the life buoy of a lie touting they have a cure for her cancer. Mom is desperate to believe in anything that will save her.

Me too.

I want Mom to live. I accompany her on all her wild goose chases. And I beg God daily to let her live. Mom probably begs God too. Both of us spend a lot of time drowning in false hope and crying out to God in prayer as each precious day passes and the clock of my mother's life counts down the minutes.

Today Mom emerged from her bedroom frustrated. It's not the first time. Every day she grapples with her faith in a constant tug of war. I can only imagine the battle raging within my mom today. It's probably much fiercer than the battle raging inside myself. Today Mom is really angry at God.

"You said God answers prayer!" Mom vehemently spits her words at me from across the room.

"I prayed for your father and laid hands on him while I was riding with him on the motorcycle!" Mom screams recalling a memory from decades ago. "But God never answered my prayer!"

Mom pauses and stares at me in accusation awaiting my answer to her unspoken "why". For whatever reason she always seems to think I have an answer for why God does or doesn't.

"I prayed God would change your father's heart and make him a godly man!" She continues in her torrent of accusations against God while glaring at me as though I represent Him.

The hurt and frustration I hear in her voice makes me feel helpless. Because I have no answer. I don't know why God doesn't answer her prayers.

I do remember the day my mom speaks of because it was only a few months after her motorcycle ride with my father when he left her. And us. For good. Dad finally made good on all his threats over the years and walked out the door one last time. I'll never forget how my baby sister clung to his leg begging him not to leave. That definitely was not the answer from God Mom was looking for. And then, to add insult to injury, within six months of their divorce, in November 1976, Dad married another woman.

Yes…definitely not the answer mom wanted.

I guess I'd be angry at God too.

Twenty-one years have now passed since their divorce. But Mom hasn't forgotten what God didn't do. And she's held on tightly to her bitterness and unforgiveness.

Toward my father…and toward God.

"God never answered me." Mom repeats as she fades into the floor in a weeping puddle of brokenness.

My eyes fill with tears. I wish I had her answers. I wish God would whisper the answers to her questions in my ear. Or give me words to comfort and help my mother. But God is silent.

I guess He isn't listening to me either.

All I can do is try to get through each day, as best I can, and watch her die.

November 7, 1997

I'm in the kitchen finishing up the dishes when my sister Kathy screams from Mom's bedroom. I race down the hallway to see what's wrong and find Kathy kneeling and sobbing at Mom's bedside while holding Mom's hand. When I enter the room

Kathy looks up to me in agony.

Mom is taking her last breath.

Kneeling down I take Mom's hand in my own as tears stream down my face. In a few moments time, Mom's breathing stops and her body becomes still.

Mom's been in a comatose state for the past seven days. Eight days ago, she was laughing, telling jokes, sharing stories and visiting with her children and grandchildren one last time. But then her cancer reared its evil head and reached in and grabbed hold of Mom's heart and mind. And refused to loosen its death grip on her life. Within days the cancer traveled through my mother's body ravaging and destroying any healthy pieces she had left. It was relentless. In the end, cancer finally took away the last of who she was. And showed no mercy while doing so.

But today God has been merciful. He has taken her home quickly. He hasn't allowed her to continue to suffer or linger in pain. I watch from her bedside as Mom's face softens and a strange, wonderful peace enters the room. And then I smile at a revelation.

She's in God's arms now.

Kneeling beside her I can almost feel my nose pressing up against the window pane that separates this world from the next. The spirit world feels so close. The closest I've ever come to it this side of heaven. I have no doubt where Mom is as I turn to my sister who is weeping beside me.

"She's in the arms of Jesus." I smile through my tears.

I can feel it. I know it. I'm absolutely sure of it.

But my sister is beside herself. She's lost in an abyss of deep sorrow. She continues to sob. My revelation doesn't bring her any comfort. Because she doesn't believe in God or heaven. So she is without hope. But I've never been more certain about anything in my entire life. I know exactly where my mom is.

Nine Months Later
August 1998

It's early Sunday morning. The phone rings. I rush to answer so it doesn't wake up my two sleeping children. When I answer I hear someone crying on the other end. It takes a moment before I realize it's my father.

"Hi honey." His words are barely audible.

Why is my father crying?

"Hi dad." I can barely understand what he's trying to say. "Are you ok?"

"I'm great honey." Dad answers before continuing. "I gave my life to Christ today." He's starts sobbing. He can barely get his words out. "It feels wonderful! I've never been this happy in my entire life!"

Wow.

I've been seeing small changes in my father over the past few months…but this? The tears slowly begin to cascade down my face. This? …This, is a miracle.

I turn my face upward, toward heaven, unable to fathom what God has just done. How could God take an adulteress, alcoholic man, who physically abused his children, and transform him? How could God succeed in taking an angry, bitter, old, unforgiving man and made him brand-new? Like a bright, new, shiny penny.

I listen to my father cry quietly on the phone and I can't help but smile through my own tears. How can anyone possibly deny God's existence when He so completely transforms the life of someone like my father? There is no earthly explanation for what has just happened in my father's life.

But God…

A memory of my mom is triggered and springs to life in my memory. What she said nine months ago comes flooding back into my heart. I remember back to how Mom told me she'd laid hands on my father's back and prayed for him, when she was riding with him on the back of a motorcycle…all those years ago. I recall Mom telling me she'd prayed God would change my father and make him into a godly man...And I also remember how, in the last days of her life, Mom had questioned God's existence and His ability to answer her prayers…

I catch my breath as a deep humility flows over me and fills me. To think that, nine months after Mom's death, I'm the one witnessing God's answers to my mother's prayers. Prayers Mom prayed during her lifetime that God chose not to answer, until after her death. I'm truly humbled by the goodness and faithfulness of God. He is a God who has no time restraints on prayer.

I wonder if she can see us from heaven? I wonder if she can see what just happened in my father's life today?

I sigh to myself.

...If only she could have been the one who answered the phone this morning...

...If only she could have been the one who heard my father's tearful proclamation...

...If only she could have been the one to feel her heart burst with joy, as mine is now...

If only…

Someday I'll tell my father how my mom prayed for him. But not today…today belongs to my father and God.

June 1999

Northern Michigan is gorgeous this time of year. The warm summer sun is a welcome change after the cold, dreary days of winter and gray days of spring. Out of the 365 days that make up a year, Michigan typically has only 70 clear, sunny days. Lucky for me, today is one of those days.

The little park in Downtown Mackinaw City I'm currently sitting in, has always been a favorite of mine. The view of Lake Huron never disappoints me. Today the sun bouncing off the water looks like bursts of tiny diamonds sparkling brilliantly in the sunlight. I take a deep breath and inhale the moist air around me.

Oh, how I love the smell of water…and Michigan summers! I proclaim to my heart.

I'm enjoying the warm sunshine and watching the children who are playing in the park. They're playing Freeze Tag which was one of my favorite games as a child. Amongst the playgroup is a red-headed little boy and girl. The color of their hair reminds me of my own two children who happen to be waiting for me back at the campground. It won't be long until my husband picks me up from the park so I can get back to our trailer in time to make supper.

My journal is sitting next to me on the park bench. It's journal number three in my son's stack of journals. I've been writing to him since the day he was born...nine years ago.

I pick up the journal, flip it open and begin reading a random entry to pass the time as I wait for my husband. The entry happens to be the one I wrote on October 7, 1997...almost two years ago. A journal entry I've long forgotten. As the sun keeps me warm from the cool breeze coming off the water, I begin to read...

October 7, 1997 5:15 a.m.

For some reason I can't sleep. I'm worried about my mom. I've been worried about her all week. She's been so weak and her ankles are so swollen that it's been difficult for her to get around.

I wonder how much longer she has to live.

I'm unsure as to how I'm feeling or if I'm feeling at all. Am I numb? Am I hopeless? I have so many conflicting emotions. Part of me wants to get on with this. Lie her to rest so she can have the peace and love that seems to have eluded her in this life.

But, can I let her go? Is that what this is all about...this limbo I find myself in? Part of me is ready to let her go. But part of me wants to hold on to her. I'm torn in two.

I wish things could have been different for her. I'd like to somehow erase the end of her story and rewrite her life with a better ending. And yet I'm powerless to do so. It simply can't be done.

Hers was not an easy life. The hurt and pain she's suffered through the years has caused her heart to become a dry, cracked, empty reservoir...whose only hope was in waiting for the rain...a rain that may never come in this life.

Her true happiness...true love...true peace...might be waiting for her, in death. Maybe in death the rain will fall into her soul and revive what has been crushed for so long.

I look up from reading and gaze out across the water.

I miss her. I miss being able to call my mom and tell her about my day or ask her advice about something I'm struggling with. I miss being able to cry to her when I'm sad. I miss Mom's voice and her laughter…or the mischievous sparkle in her eyes when she knows she's right and I'm wrong…

I wish she was still here.

It makes me sad thinking about the pain Mom endured in her life. And how she wasn't able to turn things around and let go of the pain, the unforgiveness and the bitterness…

Looking back down at the journal, I turn the page and continue to read.

God, I have one final request to ask of You for my mom and it is this:

That Mom might be in my home or my brother Terry's home at the time of her death. That whatever place she's in during her final hours, will be filled with the mighty presence of the Holy Spirit.

That, at the time of my mother's death, she will feel God's powerful presence and she'll feel His loving arms around her.

That, at her death, she'll finally find, and feel, the love and peace that has evaded her in this life

And finally, God, if possible, I ask that I might share her last moments with her.

This is my final request.

Closing the journal, I can't stop the tears from streaming down my face as my mind is filled with a new revelation.

Wow. Shivers run down my arms.

How do I put into words what just happened? How do I describe what God just did using my own written words?

Reopening the journal to the first empty page, I grab my pen and begin to write.

June 27, 1999

Michael, I'm fighting to try to keep my composure right now as I write to you…I just went back through this journal and read some of the things I've written to you in the past.

I'd forgotten the requests I made of God in October of

1997 when my mom was in the last months of her life. I'm thankful I wrote them down in this journal for you...and for me. And I'm thankful God took me back to those entries today...so I could remember.

Michael, God just used my own written words to remind me of how faithful He is...how He listens to me...how real He is in my life...how He truly does hear and know the desires of my heart and how He always answers my prayers. It's the same for everyone He loves, Honey.

Today God spoke to my heart in a powerful way. He used an old entry in my journal to show me something from the past. He revealed to me that on November 7, 1997, the day my mom passed away, He'd granted every request I made of Him...every request I wrote in this journal on October 7, 1997. Wow...Who but God can do that Michael?

I know of no one.

A Mother's Thoughts

How amazing is it that God showed me how He'd answered a prayer I'd written to Him two years prior? A prayer I'd long forgotten! God left me speechless and crying tears of joy that day. I was in awe of how real He is. Was it a coincidence that, on that day, I would open my journal to that particular page to be reminded? I think not.

Our prayers are so very precious to God. Even though we often forget what we pray, God does not. Revelation 5:7-8 tells us that our prayers are always before God. They are with Him in his throne room in heaven.

He went and took the scroll from the right hand of him who sat on the throne. And when he had taken it, the four living creatures and the twenty-four elders fell down before the Lamb. Each one had a harp and they were holding golden bowls full of incense, which are the prayers of God's people.
– Revelation 5:7-8

The Bible is full of stories of God answering the prayers of those who've left their earthly life. But to have a real-life story of my own to share! Wow! That's something to be thankful for! And I am.

I've shared this beautiful story many times, with many people. It's such a powerful testimony of who God is. He is faithful and all knowing. He hears us…He sees us…and He loves us. He cares about the things we care about. And He always answers our prayers in His time and in His way. Even after we die.

It's impossible to know how, and when, God will answer a prayer but if there is one area of my life where I'm batting 1000, it is this…I've never been able to figure out how God will answer a prayer of mine. In my life, God has always answered my prayers in a way that is different and so much better than I could ever have imagined. I can't help but think of a verse in the Book of Isaiah…

For as the heavens are higher than the earth, so are my ways higher than your ways and my thoughts than your thoughts.
-Isaiah 55:9 NASB

For me, this is true…100% of the time! God's thoughts and ways are always different than mine!

For those of you who may be wondering what happened in my dad's life…

My dad went on to lead a godly life until the day he died. He became the greatest prayer warrior of my life.

Each morning Dad would rise out of bed at 5:00 a.m. to go sit in his recliner in the living room. There, in the wee hours of each morning, Dad would read his Bible and pray. He rarely missed a day.

Dad kept a long prayer list in his Bible. It included many people I knew, and many people I didn't know. My name was on Dad's list. As were the names of those I love the most.

Dad knew the needs of everyone on his list. And he dedicated himself to getting up in the early hours of each morning to talk to God about each person on his list.

When my dad was alive, I'd wake up each morning knowing dad had already wrapped me in his prayers. And many times, as I went through my day, I often felt my dad's prayer blanket wrapped around my shoulders.

    Through the years I grew to covet my dad's prayers. For myself…and for those I love. And when my dad passed away in February of 2021, the one thing I grieved most…was the loss of the prayer blanket my dad had always wrapped me in.

    I still miss it. I will always miss it.

Take Aways

1) **God speaks through prayer.**
   This is the confidence we have in approaching God: that if we ask anything according to his will, he hears us.
                                                           - 1 John 5:14

   If you believe, you will receive whatever you ask for in prayer.   - Matthew 21:22

2) **God never gives up on us.**
   So he told them this parable: "What man of you, having a hundred sheep, if he has lost one of them, does not leave the ninety-nine in the open country, and go after the one that is lost, until he finds it? And when he has found it, he lays it on his shoulders, rejoicing...   -Luke 15 3-6 ESV

3) **Believers will receive eternal life.**
   For God so loved the world, that he gave his only Son, that whoever believes in him should not perish but have eternal life.   - John 3:16

4) **God sees everything we do, hears everything we say, knows everything we think and reads everything we write.**
   The eyes of the Lord are in every place, keeping watch on the evil and the good.   - Proverbs 15:3 NLT

Fall of 2020, this was one of the last pictures taken of my father and I before his passing in February of 2021.

Chapter 8

God Speaks Through Our Thoughts

For who knows a person's thoughts except the spirit of that person, which is in him? So also no one comprehends the thoughts of God except the Spirit of God. Now we have received not the spirit of the world, but the Spirit who is from God, that we might understand the things freely given us by God. - 1 Corinthians 2:11-12 ESV

Friday, April 6, 2000

My running route is pretty much the same every day. I set out running north through our country neighborhood until I reach the main paved road at the end of our subdivision. There I turn left and head south until I reach my favorite dirt road. It's the one that joins the main road about a half mile south of our subdivision entrance.

My favorite dirt road leads into hundreds of acres of swampland and forest. It weaves back and forth through the trees and makes its way deep into the woods where the only inhabitants are the forest creatures. This beautiful two-track is the most peaceful part of my daily run.

On my runs through the forest, I often spot the residents of the woodlands. Squirrels scamper between the trees and chatter at me in annoyance when I invade their quiet solitary domain while, at the same time, birds fly over me in song. Deer often graze by the side of the road ahead of me and quickly run off into the woods upon my approach.

Today as I am just about ready to leave the pavement of the main road, to turn down the dirt road, I cross paths with a man in a red car. Although it's unusual and a bit odd, I don't pay much attention to the man as I turn into the two track and make my way into the woods. Meanwhile, the man exits the dirt road, turns left and heads down the main road leaving me alone to enjoy the nature that awaits me inside the forest.

Entering the forest, I softly exhale as the serenity of the woodlands wraps me in its arms. The rhythmic sound of my footsteps hitting the forest floor has a calming effect on me. My pulse naturally relaxes as the peace of the forest flows through me and settles deep into my soul.

But within moments my tranquility is shattered by a still, small voice that enters my mind…

"Turn around" …. *"Red car"* … *"Coming back"* …

The words are few but powerful and ones I can't ignore. A gut punch sense of urgency almost knocks me off my feet. Electrical impulses of fear shoot through me from head to toe startling me. My body responds immediately and turns me around. Something inside of me tells me I have to get out of the woods and fast.

My stride quickens as my legs take on a life of their own. I start to race back down the road in an eerie, calm state of panic before doubt enters my mind to take up battle.

This is stupid.

My breathing increases and my lungs begin to cry out beseeching me to slow down. My three-minute sprint feels like an eternity as my mind continues its back-and-forth battle.

Why am I doing this?

My heart struggles to catch up with my fear. My body ignores the battle raging in my mind and continues running faster than my legs have ever carried me.

I'm just being paranoid!

Rounding the last bend in the road with only a few more yards to go, the victor in the battle for my mind seems all but certain. My doubt is the clear winner.

See…it's nothing! Just me being paranoid! My doubt arrogantly professes to my mind with certainty. As I reach the entrance to the forest, my body slows to a walk relieved the battle in my mind is over.

I knew I was just being paranoid. I admonish myself as I exit the woods and look around trying to determine which direction to take to continue my run.

And then I see it…

The red car.

The red car is coming toward me down the main road.

It's the same red car the man was driving that exited the forest as I was entering it.

Panic meets me at the entrance of the woods.

He's back!

Shivers run through me.

Why is he back?

My eyes lock with his as his car brings him closer.

What should I do?

He drives slowly past as I stand on the side of the road watching him. He then comes to a full stop at the entrance of the next road.

What is he doing?

He turns into the road, backs out and starts heading back towards me.

Why did he turn around?

My fear makes it hard for me to breathe.

Where should I go?

I look around for an escape as the man's car inches closer.

Where can I go?

I scurry over to the opposite side of the road hoping to put some distance between the man and I.

Where is the nearest house?

I look around for a place to run to but see nowhere.

Will anyone hear me if I scream? I wonder in terror as I check to see the man's progress and realize he's now only a few yards from me.

God, please help me! I scream out to God in my mind, knowing there is nothing left for me to do…but run.

And then, just as I'm about to start running...

The man in the red car steps on the gas and drives past me without stopping. As he picks up speed and heads south, a flood of relief engulfs me. When his car reaches the bend in the road, makes the last turn and disappears around the corner, I can finally breathe.

A sudden rush of adrenaline crashes into my body causing my knees to go weak. My legs resist the temptation to collapse under my body weight. I begin to tremble and shake uncontrollably as a tornado of questions and thoughts begins to swirl in my mind. And then my panic slowly begins to subside.

What just happened?

I take control of my weakened legs and stand upright.

The warning in my head! I exhale deeply and lift my eyes to heaven. *Your voice God?*

I close my eyes to the brilliant sunlight and sigh in relief trying to calm my trembling.

You warned me to turn around...but why? What would have happened if I'd not heeded Your warning? What did You just protect me from?

Overcome with emotion I bow my head. Tears fill my eyes as the truth is revealed to my heart.

Oh my gosh! You were right there in the middle of the forest with me! You knew right where I was!

Grateful tears stream down my face as I turn north and start heading home.

You saw the danger I was in...and you intervened!

I catch my breath as goosebumps run down my arms.

Keeping a watchful eye around me, I slowly begin to jog. My body feels like a wet noodle but I'm able to settle into a pace that allows me to breath more comfortably. No longer anxious, or afraid, I can't help but consider how real God is as I run toward home.

He sees me. Always. He always knows where I am. He's always watching out after me.

I can't help but think about how real God's presence is in my everyday life...and how much He loves me.

On my run home the sun seems brighter as I continue to ponder the greatness of the God I serve.

He protects me...He sees me...He goes everywhere with me...I'm never out of His sight...

Picking up my pace I make the final turn toward home thanking God.

A Mother's Thoughts

As I ran home that day, I couldn't help but think about my son Michael. He was not yet ten years old and he had so many questions about how God speaks to us. He wanted so badly to have a personal connection with God. I couldn't wait to tell him what had just happened to me that day. I hoped it would help him in knowing how God speaks.

When I got home, I shared the story with him, my husband and my daughter. Today we refer to it as "The Red Car Story".

To this day I do not know what God protected me from that day. I will probably never know this side of heaven. But I do know God protected me. His still, small voice entered my mind in the form of a thought to warn me and direct me to turn around. Thankfully I did, without hesitation.

That day I shared with Michael, how thoughts entering our mind, is one of the ways God speaks to us. I told Michael that sometimes the thought might bring to mind a person we're to pray for. Or sometimes the thought will impress upon us to call a person or to write a letter. Or sometimes the thought warns us and tells us to turn around on a dirt road in the middle of the woods because unbeknown to us, we are running deep into the claws of danger.

God does indeed speak through thoughts that enter our mind but, having said that, we must be cautious. Because, not every thought that enters our minds is from God.

When thoughts enter our minds, we must use discernment and compare what is being said to what we know to be true in the Bible. When God speaks to us, it will never contradict His Word in the Bible.

In this real-life story, the thought I was given was accompanied by a gut feeling that something was wrong thus the reason I didn't hesitate to turn around immediately. The feeling I had was a "gut" Holy Spirit feeling that I define as a powerful feeling of complete certainty that "you know, that you know, that you know." It's a feeling you can't ignore because it's a feeling that doesn't go away. It's a feeling you can't shake. You may have no idea why, but you just know... that you know...that you know. For some reason, deep in your gut, you just know it is true.

Sometimes a thought I think is from God, is not from God. Sometimes we are wrong when we try to discern our thoughts from God's. That's ok. It's all part of the learning curve. Practice is how we grow and learn to recognize and know God's voice.

At other times the thought coming into our head turns out to be true. When that happens its confirmation that the thought is indeed from God. The more we get in tune with the Holy Spirit, and the more time we spend in the Bible and with God, the easier it is to discern the voice of God.

When we experience stories like The Red Car Story, it's important to share these stories with our children as they take place in real time. The longer we wait to share a story, the foggier the story becomes and the more opportunity doubt has to creep into our minds and make us believe that what we experienced, didn't really happen.

When doubt enters our minds, we must quickly take it captive and refocus on what we know to be true. Don't let doubt rob you of the joy that comes from experiencing God in real time.

As I told this story to my family on the day it happened, I have to admit I started to feel like maybe I was a bit crazy. I started to doubt myself and what really happened. The doubt I felt was much like the doubt I experienced as I was running back to the entrance of the forest. It caused my heart to want to shrink back from telling my family the truth of what had happened. The doubt also caused me to think about what my family members might be thinking of me as I told them my story, which in turn made me want to shrink back from telling the story.

The more time that passes between our experience and the telling of our story, the more opportunity doubt has to enter into our hearts. In turn, we run the risk of not ever telling the story God has given us. That's why we must boldly speak the stories we know to be true and we must keep repeating them.

God doesn't give us stories to keep to ourselves.

In my Red Car Story experience, I already shared with you how I was given a "gut Holy Spirit feeling". That gut feeling fills you with so much certainty of what's true, that it's impossible to believe, or speak of, anything other than what you know to be true. I believe it's the work of the Holy Spirit when I experience that gut feeling.

Lord, thank You for speaking to us. Forgive us for the times when we doubt Your Voice. Thank You that You love us enough to warn of the things we can, and cannot, see. Thank You for Your presence in our lives...for Your constant protection and guidance...and for loving us, Lord.

Take Aways

1. God speaks through our thoughts
   For who knows a person's thoughts except the spirit of that person, which is in him? So also no one comprehends the thoughts of God except the Spirit of God. Now we have received not the spirit of the world, but the Spirit who is from God, that we might understand the things freely given us by God. - 1 Corinthians 2:11-12 ESV

2. God sees us and is with us where we are, every moment, of every day.
   The LORD your God is with you, the Mighty Warrior who saves. He will take great delight in you; in his love he will no longer rebuke you, but will rejoice over you with singing. - Zephaniah 3:17

3. God protects us.
   In God, whose word I praise, In God I have put my trust; I shall not be afraid. What can mere man do to me?
   - Psalm 56:4 NASB

Chapter 9

God Speaks Through the Holy Spirit

When the Spirit of truth comes, he will guide you into all the truth, for he will not speak on his own authority, but whatever he hears he will speak, and he will declare to you the things that are to come.   – John 16:13 ESV

July 27, 2000

    It's been a long, close game under the hot July sun. Our team and the local team are battling it out on a dusty, dry baseball field. The winner of this game will advance to the final game of the Little League State Championship Tournament.

    Our first loss of the season was yesterday. That loss broke our undefeated winning streak which had been a source of pride for both the boys and parents alike throughout the summer. The boys bounced back from yesterday's loss after a cool dip in the pool but today we find ourselves in a win or go home situation.

    The fourth inning is well under way. The score is currently 2 – 0. We hold a slight lead over the opposing team.

    "Strike One." The umpire yells before grabbing a towel from the belt of his pants to wipe the sticky sweat from his forehead.

    The batter drops his head and takes a step out of the batter's box to regroup. He needs a hit to keep his team in the inning. He picks up his head, looks toward the pitcher, steps back into the batter's box and repositions his feet next to home plate. Ready for the next pitch.

    "Strike Two!" The umpire shouts holding up two fingers to signal the count.

    The pitcher grins with renewed confidence now that he's ahead in the count. He takes his time getting ready to deliver the next pitch while thinking through his options. He then cocks his head and delivers the next pitch - an off-speed change up that hurls across the outside corner of home plate.

"Strike Three!" With clenched fist the umpire quickly sweeps his hand sideways signaling the out. And just as fast another batter from our team is sent to the dugout without a hit.

My husband Mike looks up from where he's standing along the fence line near the dugout, "Close game," he mouths to me. I nod and sit up straighter in my seat in the grandstand.

As our teams' next batter steps into the batter's box the hair on the back of my neck stands up. I sense an eerie presence that starts to build around me.

Dark...heavy... I struggle to find the right words to describe it.

Ominous. My human vocabulary doesn't have the words to explain what I feel or what is happening.

What is it? It's certainly not of this world. And it keeps building. Descending upon everyone in the stands...encircling the field as though...*threatening.*

I look around for clues of what might be happening. But it's nothing I can see.

The group of young teenagers that has been heckling our team for much of the game continues their barrage of distracting sneers. Parents on both sides of the field continue watching the game in anticipation of the next play. The afternoon sky is still the pretty shade of bright blue so characteristic of the Upper Peninsula of Michigan. Nothing in my human vision has changed and yet...the feeling of heaviness and darkness continues to advance and fill in the space around me.

I look down the bleachers at Mike who is immersed in a conversation with the father of one of the boys on our team.

Can't he feel it? I wonder. My spirit senses something sinister that my eyes and ears cannot humanly comprehend.

Darkness. Evil. My skin prickles and a shudder runs through me causing me to tremble. The air feels heavy...so heavy it's getting hard for me to breathe.

Is anyone else feeling this?

I do the only thing I know to do in the face of evil. I begin to pray.

God, I have no idea what is happening or what this is, but

You do. Please protect all those who are here today. Thank you that You are with us. Thank You for Your protection over all the players and their families.

As the game continues, batter after batter from both teams take their turns at the plate. And I continue to pray.

Thank You, Lord, that You are King of Kings and Lord of Lords!

At some point the group of hecklers begins to disperse.

Please keep everyone safe God.

The opposing pitcher starts throwing more balls and less strikes.

Let Your Will be done in this place Lord.

Our batters start earning walks to first base instead of hits to the outfield.

As I continue to pray, I sense something restraining the evil from its advance upon us and I wonder, could it be the power of prayer?

Lord, thank You for what You will do in the lives of all these players and their families today and in the future. Thank You that You love all of us enough to intercede for us when we are in danger.

Coming into the final inning our team still hangs onto a small two run lead.

Make Yourself known to every living soul here today, Lord.

My son Michael emerges from the dugout donned in a batting helmet with bat in hand. He's the youngest player on the 12-year-old team having just turned 11 a month prior. He is our teams last time at bat. Michael steps up to the plate and settles into the batter's box in hopes of getting a hit.

"Ball." The umpire barely settles in behind the catcher when the second pitch flies across the plate.

"Strike." A few more pitches and Michael has a full count - 3 balls and 2 strikes. I continue to pray against the darkness from the unknown place.

Lord, please keep everyone safe...the parents, the players...on both teams...everyone Lord.

The pitcher squints in the hot sun trying to focus on the catcher's sign. This pitch has to put Michael away. The game is too close to let my son walk to first base.

The catcher reaches down into the dirt between his legs and gives the pitcher the pitching sign but the pitcher shakes his head in disagreement. The catcher looks to the sidelines seeking guidance from his coach in the dugout. The coach sweeps his hand along the side of his face in response. The catcher repositions his mitt and passes along the new pitching sign to the mound. The pitcher nods, stands up straight and clutches his mitt, with the ball inside, to his chest. Looking under the bill of his cap toward home plate he lifts his left leg, winds up and delivers the requested pitch.

The fast ball leaves the pitchers right hand and sails across the infield gathering speed as it heads toward home plate. Nearing the strike zone, it suddenly changes course and spins upward toward its target. The people in the stands scream out loud in terror and surprise as the ball makes contact with the side of Michael's face before rolling to a stop behind home plate.

The heaviness breaks and the darkness shatters.

I jump up from my seat to get a better view of what is happening.

Oh no! Please God no! Tears puddle in my eyes. *Where did he get hit? His eyes? His nose? How serous is it? Please God no! Let him be ok!*

Michael drops his bat at the feet of the umpire, covers his face with his hands and cries out in pain. Blood begins to seep through his fingers and down the front of his white uniform. His coach leaves the coaching box on the first base line and rushes to Michael's side. Time moves in slow motion as others rush forward to try and help. Someone shouts for the First Aid Kit. Within minutes Michael is escorted off the field to the dugout where Mike stands anxiously waiting.

An array of emotions and feelings floods through me as I wait to find out if Michael will be ok. I am worried and yet filled with a strange peace from God. The conflicting emotions are puzzling. And I'm confused about the feeling of evil darkness that was so heavy for so long and then left instantly once Michael got hit.

What was that? Why did it leave when Michael got hit? Is there a connection? None of it made sense to me.

Word soon reaches the stands. Michael is going to be ok.

Thank you, Lord! My heart bursts in gratefulness and my body melts in relief.

It's only a nose bleed that could have been so much worse had Michael not turned his head when he saw the ball coming…*just as Mike taught him to do out in the yard earlier this week.*

The backyard lesson paid off.

Thank you, Lord… thank You for impressing upon Mike to teach Michael how to protect himself. Thank You for making sure Michael was ready. Thank You for preparing my son and for keeping him safe.

Not long after Michael gets hit in the face, the game comes to an end. No more runs are scored by either team and our team celebrates their 2-0 win in the dugout. They will now advance to the final game of the tournament. Parents gather to congratulate their sons before walking to their cars in the parking lot.

"What a game!" One father laughs and high fives the hand of a friend. "That sure was a close one!"

Mike jogs up the hill to join me as I exit the stands.

"He's ok." He looks into my eyes and answers the worry he sees in my heart. "Just a bad nose bleed." He quickly changes the subject. "Can't believe we made it to the final game!"

A turbulent sea of emotions rolls over me as the two of us wait for Michael to join us. I'm thankful Michael is ok but so troubled by my experience with the heavy darkness.

The heaviness is gone. That was SO strange. What was that all about?

Questions continue to pummel my mind.

Where did that feeling of evil come from? And why did it leave as soon as Michael got hit by the ball?

Reality dawns on me. *What would have happened to Michael if I hadn't been praying?*

Fear slithers down my spine as I consider the reality of the what ifs.

I want to tell Mike what I experienced during the game but it seems like an impossible task. It was such a weird experience. One not of this world. How can anyone begin to understand something that I don't even understand...something that I can't even begin to describe?

A few minutes later Michael climbs up the hill from the dugout and saunters over to us stopping within an arm's reach of me.

"Great game Michael! How does your face feel?" Mike jokes as he brushes aside the hair from Michael's brow to get a better look. "I see you got a little bruising going on."

"Are you ok?" I search my son's eyes.

"I'm fine," Michael mumbles as we turn and walk toward our van in the parking lot. "Just a little black and blue."

Michael reaches the van first. He's strangely quiet as he swings open the back door of the van and begins loading his baseball gear. I can see something is troubling him.

Our daughter Lindsey runs up from the outfield fence having just left her friends, all of whom are sisters of the players, "Can we go swimming when we get back to the campground?"

"Of course! No more games until the big game tomorrow!" Mike proudly announces to all within ear shot.

Michael finishes loading his gear then turns to me with a puzzled look on his face. "Mom, I had a feeling he was going to hit me...it was weird...it was the strangest feeling...Somehow, I knew he was going to hit me. How did I know that?"

Something in my spirit leaps and tears spring into my eyes. I know the answer to his question. I know exactly how he knew the ball was going to hit him. And the truth of what I'm about to tell him leaves me in awe.

"Michael, you always ask me how God speaks to us." I struggle to maintain my composure. "The Holy Spirit - God's Spirit – can speak directly to our spirits. I believe it was most likely the Holy Sprit who spoke to you."

"Sometimes the Holy Spirit tells us things we can't see or understand. Sounds like the Holy Spirit spoke to you in the batter's box and warned you of what was coming." Inside I whisper a silent prayer to God thanking Him once again for His protection over my son before turning back to meet Michael's eyes.

"And I believe that your dad teaching you to turn your

head earlier this week while he practiced with you in the backyard was how God made sure you'd be ready for what was coming today." My voice trembles as I struggle to fight back the tears.

Michael is silent as he tries to absorb what I'm saying.

"Isn't it amazing how God protects us?" I profess with tears in my eyes, so grateful to God. "He protects us from so many things."

"Michael, I think that one day when we're in heaven, face to face with God, we'll know everything He did in our lives...things we had no knowledge of at the time. We'll see all the ways He protected us, guided us, equipped us...it's pretty amazing to think about."

As I watch Michael process what I've shared, I wonder if I should tell him about my own experience. My battle with the darkness in the stands during the game...before he got hit. It would be another opportunity for him to learn about how God speaks and works in our lives.

"When we get back to the campground, I have something I need to share with you Michael. I need to tell you what I was experiencing in the stands during those moments when God was speaking to your heart on the baseball field."

A Mother's Thoughts

To this day I do not know what that feeling of dark heaviness was that I experienced on that day. I'd never experienced anything like it before, nor have I experienced anything like it since. I do believe that on that summer day, long ago, on the baseball field, God made known to me something that existed in the spirit world that I was unable to see with human eyes. Something that was dark and sinister...and evil. Something that compelled God to strongly impress upon me the need to pray.

At the same time, while I was praying against a sinister darkness from an unknown source, God was speaking directly to Michael. I do not know how, or even if, the two experiences were somehow connected. But it is something I hope to ask God about someday.

For many years, before that game, Michael had been searching for answers as to how God speaks. In that moment at the baseball game God responded to Michael's deep desire to know Him. He gave Michael a firsthand experience of how He does indeed speak to those who want to know Him. I believe that God did this to not only protect Michael but so that Michael would always have that moment in his life to look back on. A moment when he knew…that he knew…that he knew…that he had heard God's voice and God had spoken directly to him.

My son has never forgotten that day…the day the Holy Spirit spoke to him. He has never forgotten what it felt like, to know with certainty, what was about to happen to him in that batter's box. He is still in awe of what God did that day. It is an experience he will never forget.

God knows how to effectively communicate to each one of us so we can hear Him. He uses ways to speak to us that are personal and tailor made especially for us. On a summer day long ago, in the middle of a baseball game, God spoke to a little boy in a batter's box, in a way that would impact his life forever.

Take Aways

1. **God speaks through his Holy Spirit.**
   When the Spirit of truth comes, he will guide you into all the truth, for he will not speak on his own authority, but whatever he hears he will speak, and he will declare to you the things that are to come.   - John 16:13 ESV

2. **God hears us and is with us always.**
   Then he said to me, "Fear not, Daniel, for from the first day that you set your heart to understand and humbled yourself before your God, your words have been heard, and I have come because of your words.   - Daniel 10:12 ESV

3. **God protects us from the evil of this world and the evil in the spirit world that is invisible to us.**
   But the Lord is faithful. He will establish you and guard

you against the evil one.   - 2 Thessalonians 3:3 ESV

No weapon that is fashioned against you shall succeed, and you shall refute every tongue that rises against you in judgment. This is the heritage of the servants of the LORD and their vindication from me, declares the LORD.
       -Isaiah 54:17 ESV

4. God prepares us for what is ahead.
Finally, be strong in the Lord and in his mighty power. Put on the full armor of God, so that you can take your stand against the devil's schemes. For our struggle is not against flesh and blood, but against the rulers, against the authorities, against the powers of this dark world and against the spiritual forces of evil in the heavenly realms. Therefore, put on the full armor of God, so that when the day of evil comes, you may be able to stand your ground, and after you have done everything, to stand. Stand firm then, with the belt of truth buckled around your waist, with the breastplate of righteousness in place, and with your feet fitted with the readiness that comes from the gospel of peace. In addition to all this, take up the shield of faith, with which you can extinguish all the flaming arrows of the evil one. Take the helmet of salvation and the sword of the Spirit, which is the word of God.   - Ephesians 6:10-18

5. God gives us wisdom.
> *If any of you lacks wisdom, let him ask God, who gives generously to all without reproach, and it will be given him.*   - James 1:5 *ESV*

6. God gives us powers of discernment.
> *But solid food is for the mature, for those who have their powers of discernment trained by constant practice to distinguish good from evil.*
>   - Hebrews 5:14 ESV

Michael rounding third base after hitting a home run at the Little League State Championships in Norway, Michigan in July of 2000.

Chapter 10

God Speaks Through Discernment

The person without the Spirit does not accept the things that come from the Spirit of God but considers them foolishness, and cannot understand them because they are discerned only through the Spirit.

- Corinthians 2:14

September 2014

The cool September wind hinted that winter was coming as Lindsey made her way across campus. As far as Lindsey was concerned, nothing compared to the beauty of a Michigan Fall. Fall was her favorite time of the year. The tapestry of beautiful, vibrant colors always left her breathless.

She smiled in anticipation of the coming weekend. No classes to attend. No practice. And no homework. The perfect trifecta could only mean one thing…it was going to be a great weekend. And she couldn't wait for it to begin.

The university students had moved into the dorms two weeks ago. They had resembled a train of ants as they marched single file in and out of the four-story buildings unloading all their earthly possessions. For many, move in day was the beginning of a host of firsts. The first time away from home, their first escape from the probing eyes of parents and their first taste of freedom from a lifetime of imposed childhood rules. A mixture of exhilarating emotions flowed through them as they unpacked each box…elation, giddiness, anxiety, fear…but most of all excitement. They couldn't wait to experience this new world…college life. They had dreamed of this for months. And now the long-awaited chapter had arrived. A new school. New classes. New friends. New beginning. And most importantly new freedom. Saying goodbye to their parents and their parent's last-minute words of wisdom couldn't come fast enough.

In the days ahead New Freedom would take on a life of its own. In those goodbye moments the students were clueless to the plans New Freedom had in store for them. With New Freedom would come new responsibility. All the young students' choices and decisions would now rest squarely on their inexperienced shoulders. Along with the consequences of those decisions. And in the days ahead they'd often find themselves struggling to stand upright under the crushing burden of their New Freedom.

Lindsey turned her face into the full sun and let out a sigh as she walked down the length of the sidewalk leading to the front entrance of her dorm. It was going to be a great year. She was looking forward to her last year at Davenport University.

It had been a long first few weeks of classes and hard practices. Her softball coaches had pushed her teammates hard trying to get a jump start on the new season. Her leg muscles screamed in protest as she took the stairs to her dorm room three floors up. Like all the rest of the student athletes, she'd been looking forward to the weekend. There would be lots of time to relax, unwind and chill with friends.

Lindsey opened the door to her dorm room and threw her backpack on the frumpy green sofa that sat center stage in the living space she shared with her three suitemates. The newscaster on the television, that sat in the corner of the living area, was telling listeners that it would be a full moon tonight with Indian summer like temperatures. A perfect night for an outdoor party.

Lindsey had heard the lacrosse team was having a party tonight. The team lived in a big old house a country mile down the road from campus. Right next door to the University South Apartment Complex. The students called it USouth. Most of the university athletes who didn't live in the dorms, lived at USouth. Lindsey's brother Michael had lived there his senior year. He'd played baseball for the university. Lindsey and her best friend Deb had spent a lot of time with Michael and his teammates at USouth over the years. As a result, they'd know most everyone at the party tonight. They couldn't wait for the night to begin.

***

Luck found Lindsey and her best friend Deb a great parking spot underneath a lamp post at USouth. Pods of athletes from every university team filled the parking lot and spilled over onto the adjoining lawn of the lacrosse house. Students lingered in doorways talking amongst themselves while keeping an eye out for newly arriving friends. Male and female voices shouted out hellos to those making their way toward the gathering crowd. The parking lot was filled with laughter and friendly chatter as university athletes joked with one another and took bets on whose team would rise to the top of the conference during the coming year. Every apartment door at USouth stood wide open signaling all were welcome.

Lindsey opened her door and got out of the car with a huge smile on her face. She took in the scene and then turned to Deb exiting the car from the passenger side. "It's good to be back."

"Sure is!" Deb pumped her fist in agreement. Another year of school and softball! And tonight, was going to be a blast! They couldn't wait to find their friends and catch up on the latest.

The girls walked through the door of lacrosse house at 11 p.m. Fashionably late for a Friday night. No real college party ever got going before 10 p.m.

The lacrosse house was packed. Music blared from the high wattage speakers in the great room. The thumping bass notes of each song shook the walls before escaping the house and bouncing back and forth between the neighboring apartment buildings. Students spoke in raised voices trying to be heard over the well-known lyrics being sung by one of their favorite country music stars who was singing about loving a bar...

"I love this bar, It's my kind of place, Just walkin' through the front door, Puts a big smile on my face"...

As soon as the song ended another began. All night long the music had fluctuated between country, rock, rap and the year's top 40.

The kitchen counter overflowed with mixers and empty bottles of vodka, whiskey and rum. A tapped keg sat in the corner in a tub of ice surrounded by students waiting their turn for a refill. The sweet smell of weed meandered down the stairway from the second floor. The party was in full swing.

In the midst of the controlled chaos, camaraderie and school pride took center stage. The party goers might play on different school teams, but they all wore the same colors – black and red. As far as they were concerned, it was all for one and one for all! Panther Pride!

The girls had an hour to kill before meeting up with their teammates. They would be hard pressed to have enough time to connect with everyone present given all the news there was to share.

Every circle of athletes gathered throughout the house were confident that it was going to be a great year. The university coaches had all done some heavy recruiting. The student athletes were pumped in anticipation of what the upcoming season would bring and the success that would be theirs. All were hopeful that their team would bring home a conference championship trophy.

The softball team had come close last year. Lindsey at first base and Deb as catcher. This year their team would be the one to beat. They had a tough lineup both on the field and in the batter's box. They were certain that if their team put in the hard work this season, they would bring home the conference championship at the end of the year.

It was almost midnight before Lindsey and Deb went in search of their teammates.

"That sure was a great game last week." One rugby player bragged to another as the girls passed by on their way to the back door of the lacrosse house. "That goal you scored was sick!" "Sick" being the term everyone used these days to describe something that was outstanding or awesome.

The two girls exited the house and walked quickly across the yard to the rotting back yard fence.

"They said they'd be hanging out at USouth. Let's take the shortcut." Lindsey suggests as she steps through the hole in the wood fence before emerging on the other side, within steps of the USouth Parking Lot.

"Which apartment?" Deb laughs as she follows Lindsey through the fence opening barely missing getting her arm cut open by a rusty nail.

"Not sure." Lindsey stands up straight and brushes the cobwebs off her arms and legs. "We'll find them."

"Quite the entrance we're making!" Deb jokes as she joins her friend.

Lindsey can't help but laugh at Deb's joke before something in her gut stirs in warning. Her eyes quickly do a sweep of the busy parking lot before coming to rest on a guy she's never seen before. Dark complexion. Average height. With darkness in his eyes.

Lindsey stops laughing.

Others in the crowd catch her attention. Rough looking guys interspersed amongst the student athletes. Red flags go up in her spirit.

Something feels off. She says to herself as the feeling in her gut intensifies.

"We have to get out of here." She turns to warn Deb as fear flashes down her spine.

"Why?" Deb is having a great time and she isn't ready to call it a night.

"I don't know." Lindsey can't shake the feeling. The sense of urgency. "Something doesn't feel right. We have to get out of here…NOW!"

As the last word spills from Lindsey's lips, the entire scene in front of her explodes. A tornado of violence touches down and tosses the mass of students into complete chaos. Fights break out and people begin screaming and shouting. Anger and hate cut through the crowd in a serrated path of destruction. Sounds of bottles breaking and students screaming in fear and confusion suddenly fills the parking lot. And terror fills the faces of those who, only moments ago, were laughing and joking amongst themselves.

Many students follow their first instinct and run from the melee in a desperate attempt to find a means of escape. Others have no choice but to defend themselves against the eruption of evil all around them.

Lindsey's eyes open wide as saucers as the bad feeling in her gut increases. She can't believe what she's seeing. Things are getting really bad…really fast.

"Let's get out of here!" She yells to Deb while trying to remember where she parked the car.

Which way should we go? Lindsey thinks to herself trying to figure out the best route.

"This way." Lindsey spots a cement overhang connecting two of the apartment buildings across the parking lot. The overhang will provide cover. Safety.

Across the parking lot the two girls run, ducking and dodging, trying to reach the overhang safely. Sidestepping danger as they go.

Lindsey's foot hits something that causes her to stumble. She knows better than to look down.

God, please get us get out of here! Lindsey starts to pray when she hears a window shatter. *God, please help us!*

Deb reaches the safety of the overhang first. She ducks under cover just as a beer bottle sails past, barely missing her head, as it flies between the two girls. Lindsey is just steps from the overhang when hands reach out and shove her hard from behind causing her to fall forward into Deb sending both girls stumbling toward an open apartment door.

Why would someone push us into this apartment? The question flashes through Lindey's mind as she fights to maintain her balance. The alarming thought that follows comes to her like a lightning bolt. Being shoved into an unknown apartment door could mean an even more sinister kind of danger.

Fear forces her feet to a full stop just outside the apartment door. Jerking her red head around, with fists up to her chest, she turns ready to fight the threat lurking behind her.

"What the ----." She screams boxing her right fist forward, all five foot six of her ready to defend herself until she turns and sees her attacker.

He's ginormous. The largest guy she's ever laid eyes on. Her eyes shoot upward sizing up her enemy. They lock eyes. He towers over her by at least a foot. And he is massive. She's never seen him before. She knows everyone at school. But she doesn't know this big black man.

"Whoa!" His hands go up in front of him in an effort to

shield himself from her forthcoming accusation. "Before you say anything, I'm sorry." His eyes are gentle. "A beer bottle. You almost got hit. I pushed you out of the way."

Lindsey tilts her head puzzled and looks more deeply into the heart behind the brown eyes.

Is he is telling the truth? She wonders while maintaining her defense stance.

"Aah…. thanks." She relaxes and decides to give him the benefit of the doubt. It doesn't seem like he wants to hurt them.

Another beer bottle flies by as a bloody faced guy stumbles up to the apartment door on their left.

"Where are you going?" The big black man inquires of them seeming to want to be of help.

"We're trying to get to our car." Something about him leads Lindsey to think she can trust him. "Over there." She points to her car, illuminated by the parking lot light. It's twenty yards away and kitty-corner from them.

The huge black man glances left and then right, deciding on the safest route.

"This way." He motions to them with a sweep of his arm.

Lindsey links arms with Deb for fear of losing her. Leaving the safety of the overhang the three make a break for it.

As they run, the massive man hovers over the two of them. His enormous body becomes a shield, that wraps the two girls up in a cocoon of safety that guards and protects them as they run toward Lindsey's car.

Reaching the car unharmed, Lindsey grabs the keys out of her pocket. Her shaking hands fumble with the car key. Seconds slow walk into what feels like hours as she frantically tries to shove the small piece of metal into the door lock. The struggle with the lock brings forth a new wave of panic making them even more desperate to get inside the car to safety.

Finally, the key turns in the lock and the rusty door creaks open. Lindsey hits the door lock hard unlocking the passenger side so Deb can enter.

Out of breath, but safe from the chaos, Lindsey finally turns to the big man in gratitude of what he has done.

"Thank …" He's gone. As suddenly as he appeared, the

man has disappeared.

Where did he go? Lindsey wonders for an instant.

With no time to spare Lindsey jumps into the car. Steadying her shaking hands, she puts the key into the ignition and turns it. The engine sputters for a moment and then comes to life. Putting the car into gear Lindsey presses down on the gas pedal, her body trembling as the adrenaline continues to pump through her. Turning the wheel to the right and then to the left Lindsey guides her beat-up white Grand Am out of the parking lot exit away from the melee. Only after Lindsey reaches the safely of the street does she let out a sigh of relief and allow the dammed up "what if" questions to flood her mind.

What if he hadn't been there? What if we hadn't made it to the car?

Her heart shudders thinking of what could have happened.

What was that feeling in my gutt? A premonition? A warning from God?

The torrent of questions continued to flow over her as she drove quickly toward the safety of campus.

Who was he? Why did he help us? Where did he go!?

She had so many unanswered questions.

***

The next day word spread like wild fire across campus. Rumors swirled about the Friday night party that turned from a night of innocent fun, into a dangerous situation, in a matter of seconds. During the dangerous twist of events someone had pulled a gun on one of the baseball players. Thankfully, some of the student athletes had intervened quickly and come to his defense. Someone had called 911 and the police had arrived on the scene before anyone got seriously injured. In the end, plenty of students had been hurt but thankfully, no one had been killed. Little did they know how close they'd all come to tragedy and the end of their dreams. They had all literally dodged a live bullet.

That night many students learned that New Freedom could be scary sometimes. The beginning of their season had almost ended with the taking of their lives. Many students walked away from the night safe, but with a new realization.

New Freedom included caution flags and stop signs that were important to pay attention to.

During the weeks that followed the midnight party Lindsey looked for the huge black man on campus. She wanted to thank him. She knew he didn't have to do what he'd done to help them.

She asked about the man everywhere she went. She inquired of everyone she knew. Who was he? But she came up empty every single time. No one knew the man she described and, in the end, he became her unsolved mystery. She surmised that maybe he was just a figment of her imagination?

But he wasn't. She knew in her heart that he was real.

She kept an eye out for the man in the weeks and months that followed, but she never saw him again. He seemed to have appeared out of nowhere, at the perfect time and in the precise moment, the two girls needed him most. And then he'd vanished. Into thin air. Without a trace.

For years the kind big black man would remain a mystery.

***

Years later the story of the huge black man would surface in a moment of reminiscing. Sitting next to her mom on the back deck of her lakeside home, looking out over the lake in the early morning hours, Lindsey shared the story of that scary night with her mother for the first time.

"There were a few times this happened in my life...times when I had that gut feeling warning me of danger..." Lindsey explained as she finished telling the story to her mother. "Times when I knew God intervened in the exact moment, I needed Him. I know God protected me that night in the USouth Parking Lot. He was the One who had that guy push me out of the way and then help get us to our car."

"Each time in the past when I've experienced that strange feeling in my gut it's always been a warning. Something telling me that something isn't right. It's a feeling that is always too strong for me to ignore." She paused and then continued.

"During those times, before I knew much about God, I

always wondered if it was God who was speaking to me." Lindsey shifted in her seat. "I know now it was." She paused again in a faraway place in her thoughts. "I can only imagine what would've happened had God not been watching over me." Tears of thankfulness formed in Lindsey's eyes as she turned to see her mom's reaction.

Lindsey's mother cleared her throat of her own tears before turning to her daughter to reveal a secret of her past.

"Lindsey, when you were in high school and college, God would often wake me up in the middle of the night." Her mother shared looking off into the distance before continuing. "I'd wake up with this sense of urgency…and the thought of you would enter my mind…along with this powerful feeling that I needed to pray. That sense of urgency often drove me to my knees in the middle of the night to pray for your protection."

Lindsey's mother paused and then drew closer to her daughter as her eyes filled with tears. "Honey, we won't know this side of heaven, but I can't help but wonder if your story happened on one of those nights."

Peace settled into the space between the two of them as they each pondered their shared revelations. Lindsey's mother was first to break the comfortable silence.

"You know who that was don't you?" Her mother asked referring to the big black man in the story.

Lindsey instinctively knew the answer to her mother's question. Her story about the big black man was eerily similar to stories she'd heard her mother tell in the past.

"An angel." Lindsey smiled knowingly as she leaned back in her deck chair.

"Yes…an angel." Her mother nodded confidently touching Lindsey's hand. "Just like it talks about in Luke 4:10, *For it is written, He will command His angels concerning you to guard you carefully.* I believe that God still uses angels in our lives today, Lindsey." Her mother's eyes sparkled with unshed tears. "I don't know the details of how, or why, or when He does this, but I'm certain that sometimes He does."

Lindsey looked across the lake as the sun peeked up over the horizon. A new day was dawning. God had once again taken up His paint brush to create another morning masterpiece. She took a deep breath in awe of the beauty laid out in front of her. And she thought back again to the night when she and her best friend Deb were rescued by the big kind black man...a night so many years ago...

> A tear found its way down the side of Lindsey's face.
> *God's angel.* She smiled to herself.
> *I always knew he was real.*

A Mother's Thoughts

Like most teenagers who don't want parents knowing their business, my daughter Lindsey didn't share this story with me until I started writing this book. One night as Lindsey was reading through some of my initial writings for this book, she turned to me with a question. "Mom, are there any stories in the journals about me and God?"

Most of my writings up to that point had been about her brother Michael.

"I'm certain there are." I told her somewhat puzzled by her question.

I had only just started reading through the pile of journals in search of the God stories that I had documented there. I knew I would find stories about her and God as I continued to read through the journals, but her question made me wonder if perhaps she could remember times when God had spoken to her.

As I pondered in that moment, God brought something to mind... "Lindsey, even though the stories aren't coming to me right now, I do remember a time while you were in college when you told me then there were times when you knew God had protected you. But you never shared those stories with me."

It was in that moment Lindsey chose to share the story of the big black man with me.

In the days after her revelation, as I wrote Lindsey's story, I asked her to repeat the story to me many times. I wanted to make sure to accurately convey what she'd experienced that night at USouth. I even went so far as to ask her to draw me a map of where and how things happened. Most of the story as I have told it in this chapter is true, but I did have to take some creative liberty when it came to filling in some of the smaller details.

Sometimes God doesn't allow parents to know things. I have learned to be thankful for that truth. Life is stressful enough dealing with what I do know. Even though God sometimes keeps things from me, I'm thankful that He takes care of those I love even when I don't know what might be happening in their lives.

If I'm being honest, I have to admit that it's hard for me to trust God with the lives of my children and grandchildren. And if I am being brutally honest with myself, I'd have to admit that I don't know if I will ever completely overcome the struggle I have when it comes to trusting God. But having admitted that, I do know in my heart that God is trustworthy. He has proven Himself to me over, and over, and over again. And even though I struggle with trusting God, I'm thankful I can trust Him.

I'm also thankful that God does not sleep. He's always at work on our behalf. And regardless of the time of day or night, it's a privilege when He calls me to join Him in what He's doing by calling on me to pray. Even though I may have no idea what might happening outside my four walls.

Take Aways

1. God speaks through discernment.
   The person without the Spirit does not accept the things that come from the Spirit of God but considers them foolishness, and cannot understand them because they are discerned only through the Spirit.   - Corinthians 2:14

   When the Spirit of truth comes, he will guide you into all the truth, for he will not speak on his own authority, but whatever he hears he will speak, and he will declare to you the things that are to come.   - John 16:13 ESV

2. God hears a mother's prayers.
   Once after a sacrificial meal at Shiloh, Hannah got up and went to pray. Eli the priest was sitting at his customary place beside the entrance of the Tabernacle. Hannah was

in deep anguish, crying bitterly as she prayed to the LORD. And she made this vow: "O LORD of Heaven's Armies, if you will look upon my sorrow and answer my prayer and give me a son, then I will give him back to you. He will be yours for his entire lifetime, and as a sign that he has been dedicated to the LORD, his hair will never be cut. -1 Samuel 1:9-11 NLT

3. God calls us to pray in times of need, no matter if it is day...or night.
   About midnight Paul and Silas were praying and singing hymns to God, and the other prisoners were listening to them. Suddenly there was such a violent earthquake that the foundations of the prison were shaken. At once all the prison doors flew open, and everyone's chains came loose.
   - Acts 16:25-26

4. God hears us when we cry out to Him and He will protect us.
   My God is my rock, in whom I take refuge, my shield and the horn of my salvation. He is my stronghold, my refuge and my savior-- from violent people you save me.
   – Samuel 22:3-4

5. Sometimes God sends angels to rescue us.
   For He will command his angels concerning you to guard you in all your ways. – Psalm 91:11

Chapter 11

God Speaks Through Circumstances

And they went through the region of Phrygia and Galatia, having been forbidden by the Holy Spirit to speak the word in Asia. And when they had come up to Mysia, they attempted to go into Bithynia, but the Spirit of Jesus did not allow them.
                                               -Acts 16:6-7 ESV

October 2018

  My flight lands in Minneapolis on time and my connecting flight to Saginaw will board in ten minutes. The Saginaw flight will be the last one out this evening and if I'm not on it, I'll be spending the night in the Minneapolis Airport.

  All the passengers on my arriving flight hustle to their feet the moment the plane comes to a stop at the gate. My guess is that we all have connecting flights to catch.

  The flight crew barely gets the door open before the first passenger hustles through the escape hatch. I quickly grab my backpack from underneath the seat in front of me, wrestle my carry-on bag out of the overhead compartment and join the rush to deplane.

  At the end of the jet bridge, I hit the ground running. My connecting puddle jumper is located in Terminal A. My flight from Las Vegas arrived at Terminal G. Getting to Terminal A before they finish boarding my connecting flight and close the door to the plane, will involve a tram ride and a lot of running. Although I don't usually use them, tonight I'm grateful for the moving walkways as I race across the airport.

  I make it to Gate A6 out of breath and with no time to spare. Upon my arrival the gate attendant announces from the podium that the flight is delayed 15 minutes. His timing couldn't be more perfect. Letting out a sigh of relief I take a moment to catch my breath and pull myself together.

My connecting flight is a small plane which only has 12 rows of four seats. That's probably why Gate A6 has such a small waiting area. I look around for a place to sit and find there aren't many seats to choose from. Many of the passengers on my flight are standing because our fellow passengers are using a number of the available seats to put their bags on. As I stand in front of the seating area trying to decide on my best course of action, I notice one of the gate agents speaking to a young lady who's obviously under the influence of some mind-altering substance.

"Let's go for a walk," the gate agent says to the intoxicated young lady who stands up unsteadily from her seat. The agent places his hand on the small of her back and guides her away from the seating area toward the walkway.

The exchange distracts me for a moment because the situation comes across as a bit odd to me.

Why is he doing that? Was she causing problems?

I turn my attention back to the waiting area where I spot an empty seat in the middle of the group. Hustling over to take advantage of my good fortune, I sit down and take a deep breath, once again thankful I made it to my gate on time. Earlier this year, after a connecting flight debacle, I was forced to spend the night in the Indianapolis airport. It was a scary experience and not something I ever want to have to do again.

I shift in my seat to gain access to my coat pocket. Pulling out my ticket I double check my flight information. With the delay my flight will most likely arrive a bit late. Using my cell phone, I text my husband.

Flight is delayed. Arriving around 11:40 p.m. Love you!

As I push "send" the gate attendant announces that boarding will begin soon.

I put my phone back into my pocket and look up to find the young lady has returned from her walk with the gate agent. She's now standing in the middle of the waiting area looking for a place to sit down. She's a bit wobbly. Not too steady on her feet.

Definitely under the influence of something. I sigh.

Her hair is dirty. Greasy. The strands of her hair stick together the way hair does when it hasn't been washed in a very long time.

When was the last time she took a shower? I wonder to myself.

And she smells like alcohol.

Her eyes are bloodshot. She's wearing dirty, old, light gray leggings that may have originally been white. Her filthy tennis shoes have definitely seen better days.

How old is she? I wonder somewhat curious about her story.

She appears to be a young adult woman but her black and white polka dot backpack is something a teenage girl might choose for herself.

Standing in the center of the waiting area, she now has the full attention of every passenger that will be on our plane. And they are repulsed. I see it on their faces. Their disdain and judgement of her is obvious.

"Would you like to sit down?" I ask as something warm begins to stir in my heart.

She gazes in my direction and finds me in her disoriented fog. "Yes," she replies a bit surprised I'm speaking to her.

"There's a seat right here." I offer patting the open seat next to me.

She sits down and something inside me opens up to her in a way that is uncanny. Something not of me. I have a weird feeling my life is about to change.

"I'm Sarah." She tries hard to focus on my face.

"Hi Sarah." I assume she's on my flight. "Are you going to Saginaw?"

"Yes," she replies settling into the seat and putting her backpack on her lap.

"Why are you going to Saginaw?" I ask trying to keep the conversation light.

She studies me for a moment before answering.

"God put me here," she states with confidence. "I'm changing my life. Living for God! He's called me to set the captives free," she announces to all within earshot.

Her words take me by surprise. Not quite what I expected

to hear from someone in her condition, but ok…

I spend the next few minutes getting to know Sarah. Sometimes the scattered bits and pieces of information she shares are hard to figure out how they all fit together, but she's very open and honest with me.

Sarah is from Kansas. Wichita to be exact. She's a human trafficking survivor. She's being flown to Michigan to save her life. THAT gets my full attention. The trajectory of my safe little world has never intersected with anyone from this walk of life.

Where is her mother? I wonder as I begin to hurt inside for this sweet young lady who I am quickly coming to know. She looks to be about the same age as my own daughter.

"Sarah, where do your parents live?" My heart can't fathom the fact that she's here all alone.

"They're divorced. They live in Kansas. My father is an evil man." Her honestly makes me a bit uncomfortable. How much do I really want to know? A river of questions begins to float through my mind.

Who put her on this flight? Who paid for her flight? How did she get to the airport? Why is she going to Michigan? Are the people waiting for her in Saginaw traffickers?

Despite being intoxicated, Sarah is easy to talk to. The instant connection I have with her, is not of this world. It's a spiritual connection. I know that. I can feel it.

"You smell like alcohol," I tell Sarah once we're more comfortable with one another. "Sarah, why did you drink so much tonight?"

"So stressed." She looks away. "To help me cope." She adds and looks down at the floor embarrassed. Then Sarah turns back to me and quietly whispers. "Flying scares me."

"You'll be ok." I promise her. "I'll help you." My heart breaks at the fear in Sarah's eyes.

"Why are you going to Michigan?" I try to distract Sarah and get more information. I know there is more to the story. And something inside me wants to protect her. I have to make sure Sarah is going to a safe place in Michigan.

"I'm going to Teen Challenge." A flash of hope lights up Sarah's eyes.

"Why?" I want to make sure the people waiting for Sarah in Saginaw are legit. Not traffickers.

"To change my life," she shares. "I can't live like this anymore."

I take a moment and think about Sarah's drinking tonight and the things about her life she's already shared with me. "You know what I think Sarah?" Sarah looks at me…curious…waiting for what I'm about to say.

"I think you drink to deaden the pain…the hurt inside. But you know what Sarah?" She's now listening to what I have to say with her whole heart. "Only Jesus can heal the scars inside of you." I softly point to the middle of her chest.

Sarah's eyes fill with tears as she looks down into her lap. My words seem to have struck a chord deep inside of her.

"Why are you being so nice to me?" Sarah looks up to me with puzzled eyes.

"Because I'm a Christian too," I lean toward Sarah and whisper loud enough for her to hear. "And the same Holy Spirit that lives in you Sarah, lives in me too." I struggle to maintain my composure as the tears well up in my eyes.

Our tender moment is interrupted by the gate agent calling for boarding to begin. Sarah breaks eye contact with me and searches her dirty coat pocket for her ticket. Finding it, she takes her ticket out of her pocket and does her best to focus on the words. Confused, she hands her ticket to me.

I take the ticket from Sarah and scan it for her boarding position. She will be boarding after me. I decide in the moment to forfeit my position in line and wait to board with her. "Just follow me." I stand and hand Sarah's ticket back to her.

Linking myself to Sarah has now made me an object of silent scoffing amongst the other passengers. Guilty by association, I guess. But what's happening between Sarah and I is so much more important than bowing to the judgement I see in the eyes of those around us. God is in this. I can feel Him. And the love He has put in my heart for Sarah cannot be denied.

Boarding the plane, I help Sarah find her seat and then proceed down the aisle to my own assigned seat. I stow my carry-on bag and backpack, get buckled in and watch Sarah from five rows back.

But something isn't sitting right with me. And I know what I have to do.

Unbuckling my seat belt, I retrieve my backpack from under the seat in front of me and exit my seat. Making my way up the skinny aisle I reach Sarah's row and ask the person sitting next to Sarah if he'd mind switching seats with me. He's more than happy to oblige. Sarah's face lights up when the man gets up and I plop down in the seat next to Sarah.

"Mind if I sit here?" I ask with a smile while stowing my backpack under the seat in front of me.

"You're going to sit with me?" Sarah's smile grows brighter.

I nod.

"Thanks!" She's visibly relieved that I've chosen to sit next to her.

As the pilot begins to taxi down the runway and the plane lifts up into the sky, it's obvious how frightened Sarah is of flying. She's not only scared…she's terrified. During the flight, she asks the airline attendant for a shot of vodka multiple times. I know she's looking for a way to deal with her fear. Each time Sarah asks the attendant for a shot of vodka, he looks to me for help. It's obvious to all that Sarah has had enough to drink. To the flight attendant's relief, I come to his aide and intercede by telling Sarah "no" each time Sarah signals him for service.

"He's not going to help you destroy your life, Sarah," I reason with her at one point. "You have to draw a line in the sand of your life." I implore her. "This is a new beginning for you." And then I ask her the question that has just interrupted my thoughts. "Sarah, do you love God or vodka more?"

"God." Sarah answers without hesitation.

"Then you have to choose." I surmise. "God or vodka."

Sarah looks me in the eye for a long moment and nods. She understands her choices.

As the flight continues, I realize Sarah is not only nervous about the flight, but she's also nervous about her upcoming meeting at the Saginaw Airport in an hour. During the flight, after searching through her pockets, Sarah found she's lost the contact information for the people she's supposed to meet when we arrive in Saginaw.

"Do you think they'll be at the airport?" Sarah asks for the umpteenth time looking to me for reassurance.

"They will be there Sarah." I assure her once again. But I'm feeling less than confident. What if they aren't there?

I can't leave her at the airport in the middle of the night by herself. What if I have to take her home? Does God expect me to take her home? What will my husband say? Will he agree to that? And if I do take her home, what then? I look upward for direction. *God what am I supposed to do?*

During the plane ride I learn a lot about Sarah. She was once married to a man who abused her. She's had four children, two of which died...one whose name is tattooed on her chest. I'm curious as to how her children died, but decide it's probably better not to ask.

"I got my first tattoo when I was 14." Sarah states as she proudly rolls up her sleeve to show me her name tattooed on her left wrist.

Sarah also had a 68-year-old boyfriend who abused her. She's been charged with domestic abuse four times. Throughout our flight, as the bits and pieces of her life tumble out, I'm often confused as to the order in which things have happened. I suspect the domestic abuse charges were related to her 68-year-old boyfriend.

Sarah shares that the fourth time she'd been charged with domestic abuse, she'd been put in jail for nine months. From what I could piece together, it sounds like she'd recently been released and someone was waiting to kill her when she got out of jail. And then somehow, someone put her in touch with a women's human trafficking rescue group who contacted Teen Challenge in Saginaw. My guess is the rescue group bought Sarah the $500 plane ticket and safely got her out of town.

At some point in her life, Sarah had also been raped "by a big huge black man" who beat her up and broke her arm.

"I thought he was going to kill me," Sarah says

nonchalantly as she unzips the polka dot backpack on her lap. Inside the backpack I spot a pair of shorts, a pretty purple box and a package of Red Marlboro cigarettes.

"I have PTSD from the rape, "Sarah shares as she opens the pretty purple box that I now see is filled with pill bottles. "That's what all the pills are for."

Seeing the contents of Sarah's backpack reminds me of the bagels, cream cheese and lunch meat I have in my backpack. And something makes me wonder if Sarah is hungry. I pull my backpack out from underneath the seat and open it up.

"You have food?" Sarah asks in delight when I begin to unload the backpack.

"You want some?" I ask taking a bagel from my bag. I can see her mouth water as I use the plastic knife in my backpack to spread cream cheese across the top of the bagel. Sarah is starving.

"It's leftovers from my trip," I explain handing her the bagel. I wonder if my leftovers have been God's plan to feed Sarah all along. Sarah gobbles up the food like she hasn't eaten in days.

I fill Sarah up with as much food as I can get her to eat and then we make sandwiches for her to put in her backpack for later. During the flight I ask the flight attendant to bring Sarah several cups of coffee. He's more than happy to do so. I think he's relieved Sarah has forgotten about the vodka.

After her impromptu meal, I try to keep Sarah's mind off her fear of flying by showing her pictures on my phone and sharing stories about my family. We also talk about what lies ahead of her when she reaches Michigan.

Sarah is curious about what Saginaw is like. She asks me lots of questions which I do my best to answer. She also has trouble pronouncing Saginaw so we spend some time practicing her punctuation.

" SAG… I…NAW." I sound out for Sarah for the third time.

"S…AG…NAW." Her failed attempt at various pronunciations makes us both laugh.

"SA…GIN..AW." She tries again before falling into a fit of giggles.

Sarah has a wonderful laugh. It makes me wonder how far and few between these moments of laughter have been in her life. Sarah's joy is infectious. It makes me feel happy. And as I listen to Sarah's stories, I can't help but admire her courage. How scary it must be for her to be on this journey tonight. To be heading to a state she's never been to…and to a city she can't even pronounce.

When we arrive in Saginaw Sarah deplanes first while I get my bag from the overhead compartment five rows back. As I'm about to exit the plane the flight attendant stops me for a moment and puts his hand on my shoulder.

"Hey, good luck with whatever it is you're dealing with." His comment gives me the impression he thinks Sarah and I are close friends.

"I don't know her." I smile in response. "I just met her tonight."

"What!?" The flight attendant's jaw drops surprised by my revelation.

"I just met her," I repeat, chuckling, as I exit the plane.

I'm surprised by the flight attendant's assumption and yet, I'm not really surprised. Tonight, God built a very special, close and instantaneous bond between Sarah and I. Apparently, the closeness we share is obvious to those around us.

I make my way down the jet bridge to the gate. Stepping off the jet bridge I find Sarah sitting in the first seat closest to the gate waiting for whomever is going to pick her up. I can't help but smile at the sight of her.

In some ways Sarah still has such an innocence about her. There she is, sitting alone in an airport far from home. My new special friend looks like a little lost puppy. So nervous and scared. And rightfully so….but there she is patiently waiting…and trusting…trusting that someone will come for her…someone she's never met.

"Sarah, they aren't going to meet you here," I laugh affectionately as I approach her. "Come on." I motion to her as I walk by.

Sarah grabs her backpack, jumps up out of her seat and quickly follows me, visibly relieved I haven't abandoned her. As she catches up to me, I explain.

"The people you are meeting are not allowed past the security checkpoint Sarah. They'll be waiting for you out here." I gesture toward the doors that will take us into the waiting area near baggage claim.

Sarah and I make small talk as we walk through the double doors and into the lobby area. I speak as loudly as I can without appearing obvious. I hope that whomever Sarah is meeting will hear us and realize that I'm walking with the person whose plane they've come to meet.

Is someone here for her? I ask myself as Sarah and I continue our friendly exchange.

Will the person know who she is? I wonder as I search the faces of those we pass.

"Sarah?" A lady seated to our left, who is sitting next to another lady on her right, calls out.

I'm so relieved and thankful that someone is actually here to meet Sarah's plane.

Sarah and I walk over to the two ladies as they stand up to greet us. We all introduce ourselves. Within minutes I verify for myself that the two women are legit. The fact that they know, and have worked with the music pastor of my church, confirms that I'm leaving Sarah in good hands...and that Sarah will be safe.

"Sarah has been really nervous." I explain to Katie and Audra from Teen Challenge. "She's been wondering if someone would be here tonight."

"We're just glad she came." Katie states. The soft heart I hear behind Katie's words causes me pause as I realize that there are probably plenty of nights when she and Audra drive to the airport to meet the Sarah's of the world and no one comes off the plane. How heart breaking those moments must be for them. And then something dawns on me...

Tonight, Sarah came perilously close to not meeting up with Katie and Audra. Had Sarah stayed in the seat at the gate, where she sat down when she first exited the plane, she might have missed them both! By the time someone in the airport might have thought to ask Sarah if she needed help, Katie and Audra would have been long gone.

What would have happened to her?! Shivers run down my arms and my body trembles in response of the truth. Sarah has no idea how close she came to missing Katie and Audra tonight.

Meanwhile, Sarah's talking a mile a minute. She's also relieved that Katie and Audra are here to meet her. As I listen to Sarah's endless chatter, I can tell she's not only excited, but a bit nervous. She's talking endlessly about me and about what we did on our flight.

"Can she visit me at Teen Challenge? Sarah asks hoping she and I can continue to be in one another's lives.

"We'll talk about that," Katie answers and gives me a look that silently conveys to me, what she's unable to say out loud. Sarah has a long hard road of recovery ahead of her. She won't be allowed to have visitors for a very long time.

Sarah is too excited, relieved and happy to pick up on my sober exchange with Katie. She continues to tell the two ladies about our trip.

"She also shared pictures of her beautiful family with me," Sarah tells them before turning to me with a big smile.

"I'm jealous of your beautiful family," Sarah leans forward and softly admits to me without an ounce of bitterness in her heart.

Sarah's truthfulness, and the love I see in her eyes, causes an explosion in middle of my heart. This young lady, whom I've just met, has left her footprints in the deepest parts of my soul. I want so badly for her to be victorious in the challenges she is about to face.

I tenderly put a hand on each side of Sarah's face, look into her eyes and speak into her heart. "Sarah, you can do this. If you make better choices and change your life, you will have exactly what I have." I continue with tears in my eyes. "I only have what I have because of the Lord."

"Amen." Katie agrees as Sarah and I hug each other.

"Thanks, for everything you did for Sarah," Audra says mindful of the connection that Sarah and I have.

"It was my privilege," I answer putting my arm around Sarah's shoulders and looking into her eyes one last time.

"Now..." I start to say struggling to maintain my

composure, "...you go off and start your new life, Sarah." I try hard to smile as I fight to keep my unshed tears from falling. Somehow, I know tonight, is our forever goodbye.

I give Sarah my phone number on a little piece of paper before the three of them turn to leave. I know that, more than likely, I will never see, or hear, from Sarah again.

After Sarah, Katie and Audra walk through the lobby and exit the airport doors, I walk over to baggage claim to retrieve my suitcase mindful of the fact that Sarah has no luggage to retrieve. She came across the country with a backpack carrying one pair of shorts, a box of pills and a pack of cigarettes. Sarah came to Saginaw ready to start her new life and ready to courageously face her long uphill battle.

Sarah faced her fear of flying and got on a plane trusting God was leading her. She trusted God to help her find her way through the airport, get to the correct gates and get on the right flights. And she trusted Him to make sure someone was waiting for her when she arrived in a city she couldn't pronounce, in a state she'd never been to.

In one evening, Sarah had taught me so much.

If only I could bottle up her courage and strength, God. If only I could trust You like she does.

Walking out of the airport I meet up with the flight attendant from our plane. He smiles at me in recognition. As we walk out of the airport exit together, he shakes his head and turns to me in disbelief. "Wow, I thought you knew her." He says dumbfounded.

"Nope." I chuckle again at his misconception. "Just met her tonight at the gate in Minneapolis when I was waiting for our flight."

He laughs believing me, while at the same time finding my story unbelievable.

"That's how God works." I shrug and look up at him knowingly.

The flight attendant shakes his head again in disbelief.

"Well, you have a good night." He salutes me with his right hand and starts walking toward the parking lot.

"I think I already have!" I yell to him and laugh as he walks away.

My husband is sitting in the car at the curb waiting for me as I exit the airport. After throwing my bags in the trunk I get into the passenger's seat and shut the door. I turn to my husband with tears in my eyes unable to speak the thoughts my heart longs to share. What a wonderful night it's been. What a blessing it was. I feel more alive than I've felt in a very long time.

A Mother's Thoughts

When I got into the car with my husband, I was speechless. I couldn't find words to explain to him what had happened the night I met Sarah. This is how I usually feel after a mountain top spiritual experience with God. I usually have no human words to accurately describe deep spiritual experiences.

Little did I know what God had in store for me at the beginning of that night when I arrived at the Las Vegas airport for my trip home. Little did I know, as I was running through the Minneapolis airport, that my need to hurry wasn't about making a connecting flight. It was about being on time for an appointment God had scheduled for me…an appointment with a specific purpose, that would result in an amazing blessing.

I have so many questions to ask God when I see Him face to face one day. I will for sure ask Him about what happened to Sarah after the night we parted ways in Saginaw. I hope God was able to lead Sarah into the happy ending she was so deserving of.

I also have questions for God about human trafficking. I don't understand why He allows such evil to exist in our world, much less continue unchecked.

It's still hard for me to put into words how deeply Sarah touched my heart that night. She made me want to venture out of my safe, little world and be used by God in a new and different way. Sarah made me want to get muddy in the trenches fighting on the front lines of humanity…in the life-or-death battles. I will never forget Sarah because God used her to change me forever. She did indeed leave her footprints on my soul.

Note: Some of the details of this story and about Sarah (not her real name), have been changed to protect Sarah.

Take Aways

1. **God speaks through circumstances.** All through the Bible, God speaks through circumstances, but nowhere is it more obvious than in the stories of Jonah. Jonah tried to run away from God but God sent a fish into Jonah's life, to change Jonah's circumstances and the direction he was headed.

    Now the LORD provided a huge fish to swallow Jonah, and Jonah was in the belly of the fish three days and three nights. – Jonah 1:17

2. **Serving others is a hallmark of true Christianity.** As Christians we are commanded to love and serve others.
    Let each of you look out not only for his own interests, but also for the interests of others. - Philippians 2:4 NKJV

3. **Christians are the hands and feet of God.**
    "What should we do then?" the crowd asked. John answered, "Anyone who has two shirts should share with the one who has none, and anyone who has food should do the same. - Luke 3:10-11

4. **Faith and action go hand in hand.**
    What good is it, my brothers and sisters, if someone claims to have faith but has no deeds? Can such faith save them? Suppose a brother or a sister is without clothes and daily food. If one of you says to them, "Go in peace; keep warm and well fed," but does nothing about their physical needs, what good is it? In the same way, faith by itself, if it is not accompanied by action, is dead. - James 2:14-17

Chapter 12

God Speaks Through Prayer, Worship and Praise

"Do not be anxious about anything, but in every situation, by prayer and petition, with thanksgiving, present your requests to God. And the peace of God, which transcends all understanding, will guard your hearts and your minds in Christ Jesus.
- Philippians 4:6-7

February 13, 2023

Michael softly closed the bedroom door. He loved tucking his children in at night. Kneeling by their bedsides to say prayers and being able to listen to their little voices talk to God, was one of his most favorite times of the day. How could life get any better? He loved his children and his wife Ashley with everything in him.

As Michael walked across the living area on the way to the master bedroom, he smiled to himself. These were some of the best days of his life. Raising three children under the age of six wasn't often easy but, the day he married Ashley, and the days she'd given birth to Boone, Gracelyn and Liliana, were simply the best days of his life. Busy little ones made for a hectic life at times, but he wouldn't trade their life together for anything in the world.

As Michael passed the kitchen, a cold, dark, evil presence filled the space around him causing him to stop dead in his tracks.

What is that? He asked himself clearly unsettled.

The presence was indefinable. There were no human words to describe what he sensed. Heaviness? Darkness? Evil? He searched for the right words but found none to describe the depth of darkness that surrounded him.

What is it, Lord? He asked of God knowing it was something spiritual.

The evil presence was unlike anything he'd ever experienced before. And the terrifying part was that, along with the dark foreboding presence came a certainty that his children were somehow in danger.

From what? Clearly something was happening. Concern for his children's safety compelled him to return to their bedsides.

What's happening? He pondered as he made his way back to their rooms. No matter what he told himself, he couldn't shake the ominous feeling that his children were somehow in danger.

But of what? Was someone standing outside in the dark ready to break into their home? Was something going to happen to Gracelyn?

Gracelyn had struggled with asthma since she was a baby. He and Ashley had taken her to the Emergency Room several times when she was little. But since turning three, things had gotten better and they hadn't had to worry so much. Was this feeling that his children were unsafe, God's way of telling him that Gracelyn would have an episode tonight?

Michael entered Boones room first and knelt down to pray over his only son. Boone was sleeping soundly. His beautiful long dark eyelashes resting softly on his cheeks.

Lord, please keep Boone safe. Don't let anything happen to this little boy that holds my heart in his hands. I don't understand this feeling of evil darkness Lord. I don't understand what is happening, but I trust You God. Please keep my children safe.

Michael kissed Boone softly on the cheek and whispered goodnight, careful not to wake his young son. Boone was so intuitive. He knew his father well. Had Boone woken up he would have instantly known something was wrong. Michael's son would have seen the fear in his father's eyes.

Michael stood up and walked across the hall to the girl's room. Entering their room, he saw Liliana was fast asleep in her crib and big sister Gracelyn was sleeping in her own bed on the other side of the room. Daddy's princesses. That's what he called them. Princesses. His heart melted at the sight of his beautiful little girls. He adored them. He would always stand in the way of anyone or anything that threatened to bring them harm.

Michael crossed the room and knelt down beside Gracelyn. He laid his right hand on the soft brown curls of her little head and began to pray.

God, please keep Gracelyn safe. I love her so very much. Thank you for giving me such a beautiful daughter. Help me to be the best father I can be for her. And thank You God for always protecting my family.

Michael talked to God for a few more minutes reminding God of His faithfulness and goodness and love. Michael would always be thankful that he could go directly to God with his concerns and fears.

After praying over Gracelyn, Michael stood up and crossed the room to kneel down beside Liliana's bed. A smile spread across his face as he laid his right hand on Liliana's shoulder and looked down at his sweet baby girl.

Lord, please keep my sweet baby girl safe. Whatever this darkness is, please keep it from my children. I pray a hedge of protection around them God. Please send an army of angels to protect my little ones tonight and always.

Michael knew God was listening. Because He knew God always listened. And for some reason Michael also knew that tonight, God was calling Michael to his knees to pray for the safety of his children.

Three separate times that evening Michael tried to leave his children's rooms to retreat to the master bedroom and retire for the night. And each time Michael was unable to get past the kitchen before his spirit sent up red warning flags inside his soul. Something was threatening Michael's children. He didn't understand what was happening, but he could feel it. And something else kept compelling Michael to return to his children's bedsides, pray over them and beg God for their safety.

Finally, after praying over his children a third time, the darkness lifted and fled. Michael breathed a sigh of relief as Gods Peace flooded his soul. Somehow Michael knew that, this side of heaven, he'd never really understand what he'd just experienced, but he knew that something significant had just happened. A battle in the spirit world had been won. As Michael finally made his way to bed, he thanked God for putting a blanket of protection over his family.

February 14, 2023

Every day during the work week, while the kids were in school, Ashley worked from her home office for an insurance company that serviced homeowners. She was an exceptional employee and highly valued by her company. Just that morning her boss had notified her that she would be getting not only a huge bonus but a significant raise. As a result, Ashley was on cloud nine and she hadn't stopped smiling all day.

Late in the morning while working on her computer, Ashley had become uncomfortable in her chair. She'd been sitting way too long in the same position so she decided to change her position in her chair to get more comfortable. That is when something popped in her wrist. The same wrist she had a cyst on. The throbbing she now felt in her left arm was excruciating. It felt like she'd broken her arm and the pain made her feel like she was going to pass out.

The cyst on Ashley's wrist had been bothering her for over a year, but she hadn't taken the time to see a doctor about it. Life with three small children was always way too busy for Ashley to find time for herself. And she always put her needs last. That's just what mothers like Ashley did. Unfortunately, today was the day when her body's patience had run out. The pain in Ashley's wrist was now worse than ever. She really did need to make a doctor's appointment and get her wrist looked at soon.

Ashley's husband Michael had also been working from home all day. Unlike Ashley, working from home wasn't

Michael's normal routine. He usually went into the office to work. But today was special and working from home had allowed him the opportunity to attend their children's Valentines Day parties at school with Ashley.

"Are you sure you're going to be ok to go pick up the kids?" Michael asked looking up from his computer as Ashley entered the room.

"I'm fine," Ashley dismissed the thought she might not be ok. She had just gotten up from having laid down. She'd hoped that taking a break from working on her keyboard might help alleviate some of the pain in her wrist, but the 20 min rest hadn't done much to help.

"I can go pick them up." She responded again as Michael returned to the work at his desk. She figured if the pain got too bad, and she wasn't able to drive, she'd pull off the road and call Michael to come get her.

A few minutes later, Ashley packed up her purse and called out to Michael from the kitchen, "I'm going to get the kids!"

"Are you sure you're going to be ok?" Michael called back looking up from his desk still concerned.

"Yes, I'll be fine," Ashley answered dropping her phone in her purse and opening the front door.

Michael returned to the work at hand. He had a deadline to make. He had to finish the estimate he was working on and send it off to his client. Michael enjoyed his job working at *HeliService,* but some days he had less flexibility with his schedule than others. And today was one of those days.

Fifteen minutes after Ashley left the house, Michael's cell phone rang. He was making great progress on the estimate for his client and he didn't want to lose focus to answer the phone. He glanced at the cell phone screen after the second ring but didn't recognize the number.

It's a Florida number. He thought to himself as he considered letting the call go to voice mail. Calls from Florida were nothing out of the ordinary in his line of work. He was used to getting calls from companies, from all over the country, in need of their helicopter services.

No big deal. I'll call them back when I get done with this estimate.

But something stirred within Michael when the phone rang the third time causing him to quickly pick up the phone.

"Hello?" He answered while simultaneously pressing the speaker button on his cell phone so he could keep his hands free and continue typing.

"Is this Michael?" Asked a calm male voice.

"Yes, it is, may I ask who's calling?" Michael answered assuming it was a potential client.

"Your wife has been in a bad car accident." The caller calmly stated before pausing for a moment. "Where are you right now?"

Michael's heart skipped a beat. He stopped typing and looked from his computer screen to his phone. Did he really just hear what he thought he heard? He grabbed the phone off his desk and stood up from his chair. The caller had his full attention.

"I'm at my house in Leesburg." Michael answered trying to get a better understanding of what was happening. "Where is she?"

"She's just past the intersection of Sleepy Hollow Road and US 441. By the Five Star Seafood Restaurant." The caller stated almost too calmly.

*She was just here...this must be a mistake...*Michael's mind went to war with itself.... *this can't be real...*And yet something told him that, indeed, it was real.

"Is she ok?" Michael tried to stay calm as the reality of the situation began to sweep deep into his heart.

"Her air bags went off." The caller responded with more urgency. "You need to get here." The caller's voice was still calm but the fact that he didn't say how Ashley was, set off alarm bells in Michael's head.

"I'll be right there." Michael quickly responded before abruptly ending the call.

For a moment, Michael's world came to a standstill. Time throttled down into slow-motion gear as his brain tried to process what was happening.

*This can't be real...*he thought before his mind shifted gears and brought his new reality back into focus. Michael had to get to Ashley.

Michael grabbed everything off his desk and threw it into his backpack not knowing what he'd need when he found her.

This can't be happening. He thought to himself as he grabbed his truck keys and headed out the front door. *This can't be real.*

She's probably just been in a little fender bender. He reasoned with himself. *She's probably just fine.*

Michael ran to his truck parked in the driveway. Opening the door, he jumped into the driver's seat. His mind full of anxiety...every cell of his body on full alert.

It's probably nothing to worry about. He reasoned again. *The caller didn't seem upset. If her air bags went off, I just need to get to where she is, make sure she's ok and get help if she needs it.*

Michael threw the truck into gear and quickly backed out of the driveway before racing down the short road that led out of the subdivision to Radio Road. Radio Road would connect him to US 441. From there he'd turn right and make his way toward the intersection where the caller said Ashley was.

Michael's brain went into robot mode as a task list began to form in his mind. He had always responded to stress this way. Prioritize and execute. It's the way he'd overcome most every challenge he'd ever faced in life. He was naturally wired to lay all emotion aside in order to deal with whatever stressor was at hand.

There had been times in his life when Michael's unemotional way of processing situations hadn't served him well. But today it would provide him with tools that no other precious gift could. Little did he know how crucial it was going to be for him to take control his thoughts and think clearly in the hours and days ahead. He had no idea how important it would be for him to not give in to his emotions. His mindset would serve him well in what he was about the face.

The task list in Michael's mind continued to come

together as he turned onto US 441 and headed west. Each mile he covered brought him closer to Ashley.

What do I need to do first?...It's almost 5:00 o'clock.... School's ending soon... Kids need to be taken care of...it's a short window of time... His mind rattled through the tasks he needed to complete. *How do I make sure they're ok?... Someone needs to go get the kids from school... Mom and dad...have them go to school...have them stay with the kids until I figure this out.*

Michael dialed his mom's number. She answered after the first ring.

"Hi honey." Michael could hear the smile in her voice.

"Mom, what are you doing right now?" Michael asked in a rush of words as he pushed down hard on the truck's accelerator.

"Nothing. What's up?" The tone of her voice revealed her sense of something amiss.

"Ashley's been in a car accident. I need you to go get the kids at school." The truck jumped forward in response to Michael's hard foot on the accelerator.

"Is she ok?" His mom asked clearly worried.

"I don't know." Michael's flood of words gave away his fear. "All I know is that she's been in a bad accident. I need you and dad to go to school, get the kids and wait for me there."

"We'll get them." His mom assured him while trying to remain calm. "We'll leave right away. Keep us posted."

"Thanks Mom. I'll call you once I know more." Michael ended the call before his mother could respond. His mind boomeranged back to his task list...

Don't have to worry about the kids anymore... prioritize and execute...*now I just need to get to Ashley...figure out what's wrong...figure out what to do next...*

Michael arrived at the intersection of US 441 and Sleepy Hollow Road within minutes. Driving up to the crash scene he spots one fire truck and one ambulance, but no crash. Michael quickly pulls his truck off to the side of the road and parks in front of a fire truck.

Where is she? He questions himself, clearly puzzled by what he doesn't see. *This doesn't make any sense...that guy called me only 10 minutes ago…how could they have already cleaned up the crash site?*

There was simply no evidence of a crash.

But there is a fire truck and an ambulance so they have to be here somewhere. Michael reasons with himself.

Where is she? Michael's heart starts to panic before his mind robotically intervenes to set a new course before his emotions consume him.

Prioritize and execute… He reminds himself.

Michael jerked open his truck door, jumped down onto the ground and looked around. Still no sign of the accident.

Where is everyone? Where is Ashley? Michael's mind fights off a tidal wave of panic as desperation starts to build inside of him. Nothing was making any sense. With few options left, Michael started walking toward the emergency vehicles in hopes of finding someone…anyone…anyone who could tell him where Ashley was. But when he reaches the two vehicles, he finds them both empty. And no one nearby.

Where is she? He asks out loud. Panic rising in his voice. And then he hears something.

Michael stops walking and listens. Yes, he hears voices…off in the distance…and yet strangely they seemed to be coming from somewhere close by.

Michael looks up and away from the road. But he still can't see anyone. There's no one in sight. Other than those who drive the cars that keep whizzing past him as he stands in confusion on the side of the road

Where are those voices coming from? Michael lowered his head again in an attempt to block out the road noise and get a better listen. He closed his eyes and listened hard with everything in him, desperate for a clue as to where Ashley might be. And then finally the truth dawns on him.

The woods!

Michael slowly turned around and faced the woods. The woods on the other side of the emergency vehicles! The voices were coming from the woods!

Michael peered deep into the trees. The thick underbrush

made it hard for him to see who belonged to the voices. He knew there was a lake back in the woods somewhere. He knew that if he walked forward, he would eventually run into the lake, but the vines were so overgrown. They made it impossible for him to see anything.

Michael started scanning the woods looking for a clue as to where the voices might be coming from when he spotted something unusual. He could make out a path through the woods. And at the end of the path...

People! His eyes grew wide. *Lots of people...what were those people doing in the woods?*

Michael laser focused on the people he could make out and he spotted something that made his heart stop. It was a small bit of white. In the middle of the woods. Buried under the vines and thick underbrush.

Ashley's van!

Terror filled Michael's heart as his spirit revealed the truth. It was Ashley's van! It was in the middle of the woods!

Fear catapulted Michael forward. He sprinted into the woods following the path, he'd later learn, had been cut through the woods by Ashley's van as she sat unconscious behind the steering wheel. As Michael ran, the vines grew arms that reached out and grabbed hold of his legs making it difficult for him to run. And the thorns of the underbrush cut into his shins in a failed attempt to hold him back from reaching his beautiful wife. With each step the seriousness of the situation became clearer to him. And the fear pressed down and grabbed a hold of his lungs making it hard for him to breathe.

"Where is she?" Michael screamed at the top of his lungs.

"Where is she?" He screamed as he sprinted toward the group of people assembled in the woods.

"Where is she?" He screamed again clearly terrified.

Michael was indeed terrified...terrified of what he'd find...terrified of how he'd find her...terrified of a future without her. As Michael battled his way through the woods in a desperate attempt to reach Ashley, his life, and hers, flashed before his eyes in a sadistic display of what life would be like if he had to live life without her.

It seemed like it took forever to reach the van but within minutes Michael arrived at the crash site filled with people. Medics, EMS personnel, fire fighters…Michael's mind quickly registered ten people around the van, all focused on the person trapped inside.

Ashley…

A few in the group looked up at Michael as he ran up to the van.

"She's my wife." He whispered out of breath but loud enough for them to hear. Their unasked question answered, the few quickly turned their attention back to the task at hand.

Ashley's van at the crash site.

Everyone on the scene was working hard to get Ashley out of her very damaged van. A van that looked much like an accordion crushed into a tree and wrapped in a cocoon of vines and underbrush.

Michael made his way to the passenger side of the van trying to get a glimpse of Ashley. One small glimpse was all he needed…one small glimpse so he could make sure she was ok…so he could make sure she was still alive.

This is serious. He realized as the full weight of the

accident pressed down hard upon him. *This is no little fender bender.*

Michael fought to maintain his composure as the severity of the situation hit him full force in the middle of his chest. Hot tears filled his eyes as panic started to climb down his throat. He needed to see her. But all he could see were airbags. The van was filled with them. Especially in the front seat and the front window. Piles of shattered glass lay everywhere. The front end of the van had collapsed into itself. It was gone. Crushed into a tree. The impact had pushed the dashboard into the front seat. And somehow….somewhere…he knew Ashley was still in the van. Wedged between the front seat and the dashboard. Pinned into the driver's seat.

Michael ran around to the other side of the van in search of his wife as emergency rescue workers pulled tree limbs off the van and tossed wreckage out of the way. When he got to the driver's side, Michael spotted her.

Ashley…

The driver's side window was busted out. Ashley was slumped forward in the driver's seat with her forehead on the steering wheel. Michael could see she was conscious but disoriented and, much to his relief, he saw she was still very much alive.

Ashley must have sensed Michael's presence because, as he took his first steps toward her because she lifted her head from the steering wheel, turned her face in his direction and locked eyes with him…and then she began to cry.

"I'm so sorry…" Ashley sobbed. "I'm so sorry for crashing my van."

Michael reached his hand out to touch her and then thought better of it. Touching her, might hurt her.

"It's ok." Michael said softly trying to calm her with his voice. "It's ok Ashley…you're going to be ok."

Ashley's arm was laying at an odd angle on the ledge of the driver's window. Her left wrist was visibly snapped in two. She was in so much pain but the strength of Michael's presence seemed to immediately comfort her.

The front end of the van was pushed into Ashley's legs. It was almost touching the front seat she was sitting on. Ashley's left leg was hanging outside the van at an odd angle and her right leg was stuck underneath the dashboard. The firefighters were working hard to get the door of the driver's side off so they could extract Ashley from the van. But even the three Jaws of Life they were using hadn't been able to free her.

"I can't find her knee," the first fire fighter stated as he searched the demolished front end trying to locate Ashley's leg. "Oh, never mind…I found it…but I can't get it out. We'll just have to cut her out. Her leg won't move."

"But if I cut into the van I might cut her knee," stated the second firefighter clearly concerned as he started up the Jaws of Life blade he held in his hands.

"I'm going to put my arm up against her leg," stated the first fire fighter. "You'll cut my arm before you cut her knee. Just go ahead!"

Michael's eyes filled with tears as he watched the heroic efforts of the firefighters and realized the personal sacrifice each one of them was willing to make in order to save his wife. Ashley's eyes were closed but he could sense how scared she was. What was she thinking as she listened to them talk about cutting into her leg? She must be terrified trapped inside the van.

A chain saw like sound penetrated the woods as the jaws burst to life and went to work trying to cut through the door of the van. A third firefighter held up the vans dashboard in an effort to try to keep it off Ashley's legs while others continued to pull away the debris and underbrush that surrounded the van. The loud generator powering the Jaws of Life made it hard for Michael to talk to Ashley. When the Jaws of Life finally cut through the door, the dashboard dropped down on Ashley's lap causing her to scream out in pain. With the door finally off, the team tried once again to extract Ashley from the van without success. They'd have to try something else.

"We can't get her out." The firefighter using the Jaws of Life announced. "We can't cut the dashboard any more either. Her right leg is caught under the brake pedal."

"I'm so sorry," Ashley continued to sob to Michael, disoriented and in pain. "I started feeling light headed when I was driving. I was trying to pull the van over to call you…but I passed out…I'm so sorry."

"It's ok," Michael repeated trying to console her. "Everything will be ok. You're going to be ok. Ashley, don't worry about the van."

The biggest man in the group of rescuers was the battalion chief. He was leading the rescue team and doing all the critical thinking trying to figure out how to get Ashley out of the vehicle within the "golden hour".

The term "golden hour" is a term commonly used by rescue personnel. It's used to characterize the urgent need for the care of trauma patients. The golden hour is the 60-minute window that emergency personnel have, to get a critically injured person to definitive treatment, in order to give that person, the best chance for recovery. If treatment is not received within the precious golden hour, mortality significantly increases for a patient. As the scene unfolded in front of Michael something became abundantly clear. The team surrounding Ashley was in a race for her life.

Michael continued to comfort and reassure Ashley as best he could. He kept watching the battalion chief and the rescue team work to pull Ashley out of the van. Strangely the chief's presence had a calming effect on Michael. He found himself impressed with the chief's strength of command and the confidence he embodied. Michael had never been in the presence of a more amazing leader. And knowing Ashley was in such good and competent hands, brought Michael a bit of comfort as he stood near the van in the middle of the organized chaos. It also made Michael certain of the words he kept telling Ashley…everything was going to be ok.

God, thank You for these emergency workers. Michael whispered to himself not wanting Ashley to hear the fear and concern in his voice. *Thank You for this man's leadership…and for the dedication and commitment of the team surrounding Ashley right now.* Michael continued to pray until Ashley's voice interrupted his prayers.

"Michael…I'm so sorry." She continued to cry and

complain about the pain in her arm. But there was nothing Michael could do to help her. He felt so powerless. All he could do was pray and continue to reassure her.

The team was now in a race against time. With each minute that passed, the problem of how to get Ashley out of the van without doing further damage to her already bruised and battered body, became more crucial to solve. Michael was relieved that Ashley continued to cry and talk to him. It was actually a good sign. It made him believe that she was going to be ok. But something inside kept nagging him.

He couldn't help but wonder if Ashley had injured her neck or back in the accident. She kept complaining about the pain in her arm and leg, but he kept wondering about her neck and her back. He didn't want to ask her about them, because he didn't want to scare her, but he couldn't help but wonder if she had damage to her spine? Could she move her toes that were crammed up inside the crushed space beneath the collapsed dashboard? He reasoned that, if she complained about her back or neck, it would mean that she was in really serious trouble.

Please God, don't let her complain about her neck or back...please God, not her spine or back.

"Ashley, you're going to be ok." He spoke the words aloud with added emphasis trying to reassure himself. "You're going to be fine."

As Michael kept watching the team work to free Ashley, his mind wandered back to the problems Ashley had been having with the cyst on her wrist over the past year or more.

"Does your wrist hurt anymore?" He asked hoping to distract her from what was going on around her.

"Yes," Ashley answered still crying.

"This is a pretty dramatic way for you to get your cyst worked on." He chuckled hoping to take her mind off her pain.

His attempt at humor succeeded. Ashley laughed out loud. Her laughter was a beautiful sound to his ears and caused him to smile. It was only for a moment, but his joke had caused her to smile through her tears.

A few minutes later, three fire fighters and an EMS worker broke the back seat passenger window to gain entry into the van. The woman EMS worker got on all fours and crawled into the van then gently took hold of Ashley's right arm. The worker tried four times to insert an IV into Ashley's arm but her position behind the passenger seat made it impossible for her to complete the task. Not being able to get medication and fluids into Ashley's system made the situation even more dire. After 20 minutes the battalion chief spoke up again.

"We've got to get her out of there." The chief's voice had now taken on a much more serious tone. A tone that caught Michael's attention. The chief was no longer recommending, he was commanding.

"We still can't get her out," the firefighter explained to the battalion chief. "We can't slide her out because we can't get the van open wide enough. And the seat is not moving. There is nothing more we can do. We'll just have to lift her out but we'll have to be very careful with her neck and back."

The battalion chief agreed. They were running out of time. At this point, lifting her out was their only option.

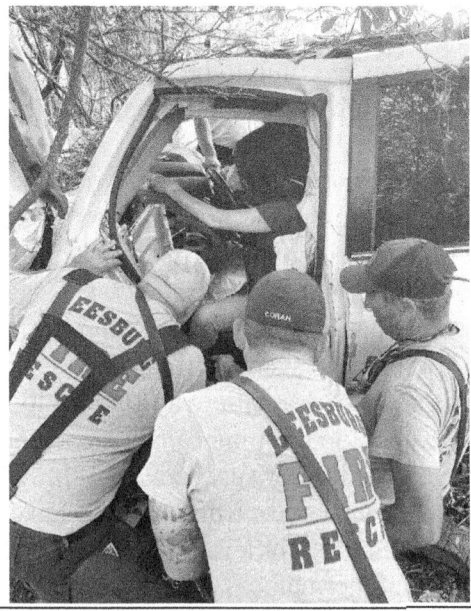

Leesburg Firefighters working to get Ashley out of the van.

The rescue workers gathered together and prepared to lift Ashley out of the van. One firefighter took hold of her belt buckles, another protected her head with his hands and a third placed his hands underneath her legs. As they began to count to three, Michael prayed.

"One…Two….THREE…" They all yelled out loudly and in unison.

Ashley's scream pierced the too quiet forest causing Michael's body to tremble and his heart to break, but strangely he was also relieved. He was relieved because Ashley had yet to mention any sort of pain in her neck or back.

As the team completed extracting Ashley from the van, additional firefighters entered the woods with a backboard. They gently laid Ashley on the backboard and fastened the straps across her chest and hips. After checking to make sure the straps were secure another firefighter placed a neck brace around Ashley's neck. The EMS worker was finally able to insert the IV into Ashley's arm and started giving her fluids. Michael moved to the head of the backboard to be closer to his wife.

"We have to get her out of here. Quickly." The chief announced again as the team prepared to carry Ashley out of the woods. "The helicopter will be on the road in five minutes."

During the time the rescue workers had worked to free Ashley from the van, other emergency personnel had worked to temporarily shut down US 441. Shutting down a busy six-lane highway in both directions during rush hour traffic had been no small feat but the local police and fire teams had gotten it done. As a result of their efforts, the incoming helicopter now had enough room to land and execute the air lift.

The battalion chief turned to Michael. "We're going to take her to either Ocala or Orlando. We're calling to see who has room for her in their trauma ward right now."

"Why are you airlifting her?" Michael asked confused. He knew there were other hospitals close by that would take less time for an ambulance to get to. "Why aren't you taking her by ambulance to Leesburg?"

"Because of the severity of her accident," explained the chief. "With all the damage, we want to be sure that, if she does have internal bleeding or organ damage, that no matter where we take her, they will have the right people and the right equipment to not only work on her, but to save her life. Orlando and Ocala are the only two air care teams in the area."

The chiefs answer had a sobering effect on Michael. Not even the chief could be certain that Ashley was going to make it. Michael didn't think Ashley had any internal damage from having talked to her, but no one could know for sure until she reached the trauma unit. Once again, the chief's strong leadership skills comforted Michael. Michael knew he could trust this man with Ashley's life. And Michael had peace knowing the chief would get Ashley to the place that would give her the very best care.

When the chief signaled to the team, the group of six lifted the backboard and began carrying Ashley out of the woods. Michael remained near the head of the backboard. Ashley's leg was stuck at an odd 90-degree angle as she laid on the backboard. She was unable to straighten her leg and she continued to cry in pain.

"Ashley, your leg will be fine." Michael tried his best to comfort and reassure his wife as he stepped over the vines and underbrush.

"I'm so sorry Michael," Ashley sobbed.

"I don't know why you keep saying you're sorry Ashley," Michael eyes smiled lovingly at his wife as he followed the team through the woods. "It's not a big deal. You are far more important than any vehicle we'll ever own."

"I feel so stupid for crashing my van," Ashley confessed to him completely beside herself.

The team continued walking forward with Ashley, carving a path through the thick underbrush. They stepped carefully through the masses of vines and twigs. Tripping and falling would be dangerous. Not only would it cause Ashley more pain, but it could possibly cause more damage to her already severely injured body.

As the team emerged from the woods, the wind picked up and the dirt from the street swirled in the air as the helicopter landed. A concerned crowd had gathered alongside the road to watch the scene unfold. An airlift was a rare occurrence. And the crowd sensed someone was seriously injured.

Two pilots exited the helicopter and made their way across the highway to the side of the road where the battalion chief was waiting. The thunderous "wop-wop" sound of the helicopter blades made it almost impossible to hear what the trio discussed after shaking hands and making introductions.

As the firefighters stood on the side of the road awaiting the chief's orders, they prepared Ashley to be loaded into the chopper. The team transferred her to a stretcher and conducted a final check of Ashley's vital signs.

"75 over 50," a firefighter announced to the team with a grave look on his face.

Ashley's blood pressure had fallen far below what was normal. Her blood pressure was now dangerously low. With such a low blood pressure the team reasonably assumed that Ashley was now in danger of organ failure and a ripple of fear ran through the group. They were unsure as to what their next course of action should be. They needed to get Ashley into the helicopter and to the trauma unit, but they were now concerned that Ashley might not survive long enough to make the trip to the hospital.

Michael was talking to Ashley when he sensed something had changed. He looked up, noticed the team had stopped moving and he felt panic in the air.

Something's up. Michael surmised. *What's happening? What are they talking about?*

Michael moved closer to the group and overheard them discussing how low Ashley's blood pressure had fallen.

"Her blood pressure is way too low," one firefighter explained to the group.

"She might not make it to the hospital," stated another firefighter clearly concerned.

Michael understood their concern but he also knew his wife's medical history.

"Hey…" Michael drew the attention of the group as he stepped forward. "I'm not a doctor but I will tell you that her blood pressure is typically low. It's usually 95 over 60 or 70. When she had our babies her blood pressure was 90 over 60 her entire labor. I'm not a medical professional but I wouldn't be concerned about her having low blood pressure."

"So, 75 over 50 isn't too far out of the ordinary then," confirmed one of the firefighters to Michael. "Well…it's still a concern… but seeing that she has normally low blood pressure, her blood pressure levels are justified, given the trauma she's just experienced."

The group breathed a sigh of relief and finished prepping Ashley for her ride in the chopper.

A few moments later one of the pilots split away from the trio and made his way over to Ashley.

"Hi Ashley. You are going to go for a little ride with us." The pilot smiled hoping to reassure her. "It's going to be ok but it's really noisy in the helicopter so we won't be able to talk to one another or hear what each other is saying."

The pilot then turned to Michael. "We're taking her to Orlando Regional." The pilot announced.

Michael nodded to the pilot and then turned his attention back to his wife.

"It's a really nice helicopter Ashley," Michael reassured her. "You are going to be really comfortable…"

Michael grinned as another thought struck him "…since I now know all about helicopters."

Ashley laughed catching onto his joke. Michael never dreamed that working for a helicopter company would one day enable him to be able to comfort his wife as she was being airlifted from a horrific accident.

Their tender, funny moment was cut short by two nurses who stepped forward from behind the pilot to take charge of Ashley.

"I love you, Ashley." Michael looked deep into Ashley's eyes trying to control his emotions. "You are going to be fine. I'm going to get the kids. I'll see you in a little while."

"I love you too," Ashley whispered as a small tear escaped and rolled down the side of her face.

The nurses took their positions on either end of the stretcher and began rolling Ashley and her IV bag toward the helicopter. The pilot followed a few steps behind. With one nurse pushing the bottom of the stretcher, and the other pulling the top of the stretcher, the nurses quickly loaded Ashley into the back of the helicopter and hung up her IV bag. Then the rest of the crew boarded and put their headsets on in anticipation of lift off. As the helicopter engine gathered speed and the huge machine began to lift off the ground and ascend into the sky, one of the nurses looked over at Ashley on the stretcher and silently gave her a thumbs up. Ashley smiled in response.

Michael watched from the ground as his wife was lifted up into the sky and he prayed a silent prayer...
Such precious cargo God...Please keep her safe.

Michael watches as Ashley is airlifted to Orlando Regional Medical Trauma Center.

Michael returned to the van in the woods. He needed to get what he could out of the van before he left to go meet his parents who were with his children waiting for him at school. He noted that several firefighters were still cleaning up when he returned to the crash scene after Ashley was airlifted. But they seemed to pay him no attention.

As Michael walked up to the van, his attention was drawn to the driver's seat where Ashley had been sitting.

She must have thrown up during impact. He surmised noting that the front seat was a mess. There wasn't much he'd be able to salvage from the front of the van.

Taking a second look at the intense damage to the van and remembering how Ashley had been trapped in the front seat, made Michael wonder anew how she'd even survived the crash. Thankfulness bubbled up inside his heart.

Michael reached out with his right hand and slid open the van door behind the driver's seat. Deflated airbags filled the space and shattered tiny pieces of glass covered the entire floor of the van. It was a miracle Ashley only had two small cuts, one on the side of her face and one on her thumb. How on earth had she ever escaped the shower of shattering glass that must have sprayed throughout the van on impact?

Divine intervention. His heart whispered. *God protected her.*

Something drew Michael's attention to the back of the van…and what he spotted there made him start to cry.

…Three empty car seats…

Michael caught his breath as the terror of what might have been exploded in his heart. He suddenly felt too weak to stand.

Through blurry eyes, filled with tears, Michael looked at the three empty car seats. All still intact. Each one secured to its own separate seat in the van. Each one waiting for the child to whom it belonged. Car seats that, on most any other day, would have held each one of his three precious children.

A painful new reality hit Michael square in the heart.

Ashley had been on her way to pick up their children...their babies. Their children had been minutes from getting into that van. If the accident had happened a mere twenty minutes later, his entire family would have been in that van. And his entire family would likely have been airlifted in that helicopter that was now on its way to the Orlando trauma unit.

Michael started sobbing. His whole body melted into a puddle in front of the demolished van as gut-wrenching sobs filled the forest. But his fear of what could have been was short lived, because God, in that moment, reminded Michael of the truth.

The car seats were empty.

Michael tearfully thanked God for what had not been. He had no doubt about what God had done. God had spared his children.

The night before, when Michael felt compelled to pray for his children's safety, little did he know what today would bring. Michael knew his children had only been spared because of the mercy and grace of God and that truth made him fall to his knees, in the middle of the forest, in awe of the goodness of God.

The firefighters cleaning up the crash site, respectfully left Michael to himself as he sobbed in thankfulness to God. All seemed fully aware of the fact that they were standing on holy ground. Ground on which God had directly intervened. Sacred ground.

What a picture of God's grace and mercy Michael must have painted for the crash site workers, as they silently watched him tearfully transfer each car seat, one by one, from his demolished family van to the safety of his work truck.

When Michael finished loading the last car seat a fire fighter approached and silently embraced him.

"It's going to be ok." The firefighter quietly told Michael with tears in his eyes. "I'm so thankful your children were not in the van. God was watching over all of you."

Michael nodded to the man, while being pressed against his shoulder, and began to sob anew. Yes...God had directly intervened in their lives and kept their children safe. Michael was positive of that. And he knew that for whatever reason, the accident was God's appointed Will for their lives.

Michael knew the days and months ahead would be hard…and there might be times when he would wonder why…but there was one thing Michael knew he would never doubt or question…the fact that God could be trusted.

Michael knew he could trust God with whatever was about to happen to Ashley and Michael knew that he would always be able to trust God with all their tomorrows.

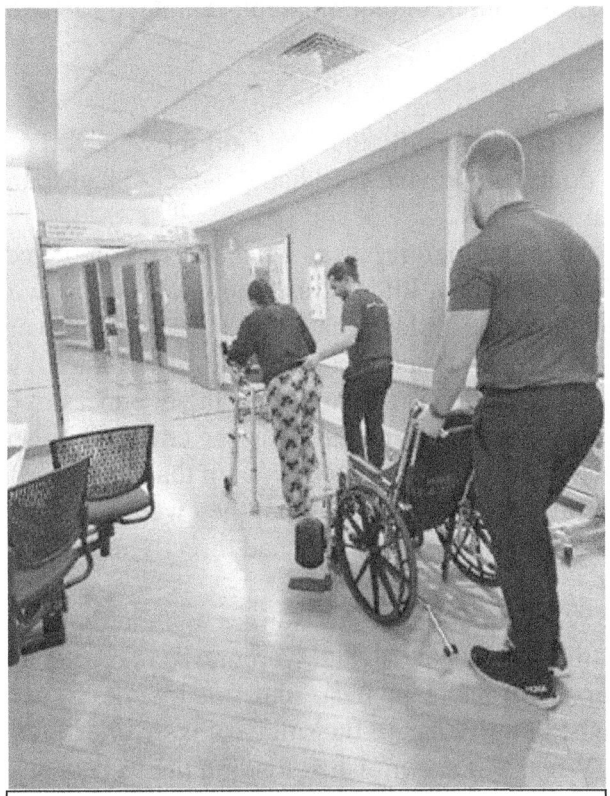

Ashley learning to walk again with help from the amazing therapy staff at Orlando Medical Center.

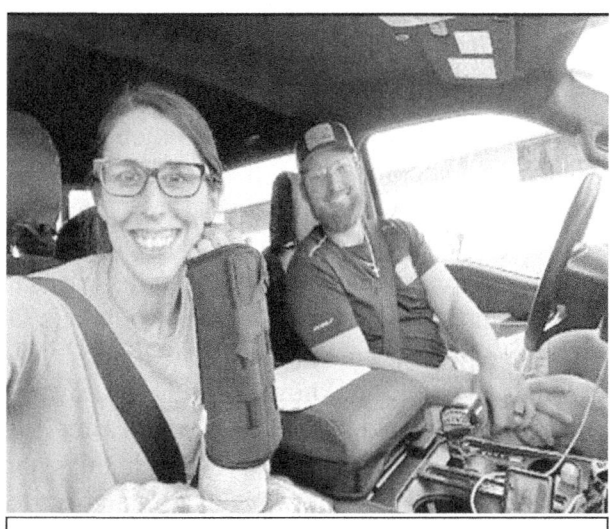

Michael and Ashley going home from the hospital.

A Mother's Thoughts

The hardest part of writing this true-life account was determining if it would simply be a story to end this book, or if this true story was to be a book of its own. The next morning after I finished writing this chapter God revealed to me that this story should indeed be a book of its own. There were too many God stories that happened as a result of Ashley's accident to cut the story short here. God willing, I will write that book one day in the future and if not me, perhaps one of them will.

If Michael had the opportunity to talk to you, he'd tell you that he believes the story in this chapter didn't begin on February 13, 2023. Michael believes this story actually began on Christmas Eve in 2022 when something very special happened to Ashley at their churches Christmas Eve service. During the service Ashley had a spiritual revival of sorts. A powerful, intimate experience with God that not only changed something in her heart but ultimately changed the course of her life. To this day Ashley and Michael struggle to find the words to describe what happened to Ashley in church that evening but suffice to say Ashley was never the same after that night.

A month after Ashley's experience in church, on January 30, 2023, Michael felt the hand of God touch his heart during a

Sunday morning service at that same church in Umatilla, Florida. As a result, Michael walked forward to the altar and rededicated his life to Christ.

I believe that both of these events in their lives set the stage for what would become a very powerful spiritual battle between Satan, his demons and God's heavenly forces. Thus, the reason why I think the Holy Spirit spoke to Michael the night of February 13th and implored Michael to get on his knees and pray for the protection his children. I believe that Michael's family was about to come under a direct attack from Satan.

Obviously, we will not know this side of heaven what was happening in the spirit world before, during and after Ashley's horrific accident. But we do know that the Bible talks about the wars that go on in heaven and the ways that Satan tries to destroy the lives of the ones whom God loves. Spiritual warfare is real in the life of every Christian.

So, what are we to do when we sense a spiritual battle raging?

When I sense a war is brewing, first and foremost, I run to God and cling to Him. I also put on the armor of God that God reminds us of, in Ephesians 6:10-18.

And I pray.

I also read God's Word out loud to remind myself, and the evil one, of who God is and who has sovereignty over my life. I have also been known to sing praise songs and recite Bible verses out loud.

I have found that Satan and his demons can't stand to hear a Christian praising God. And when I praise God and sing out loud to Him it often causes the evil one to flee my presence.

The time to prepare for battle is now. Satan is real. It's not a matter of IF Satan will attack, it's a matter of WHEN. Entire books have been written on the subject of spiritual warfare. I have read many of them. I can't emphasize enough how important it is for you to gain knowledge on this subject and start preparing for battle.

My most recent read about spiritual warfare is a book written by a friend of mine, Kelly Hawkins. After the Bible, Kelly's book entitled *"Warrior Woman: Boot Camp"* is a good place to start in order to prepare yourself for the battles ahead.

Ashley's recovery was nothing short of miraculous. She worked hard to get back home to her husband and children. Originally, we thought Ashley would have to spend months in therapy learning how to walk, dress herself, etc., but love of family is a powerful motivator when it comes to recovery. From the day Ashley was airlifted, to the day she left rehab, she only spent a total of ten days in the hospital. Boone and Gracelyn couldn't wait to take their mommy for an evening walk when she got back home to them. Their baby sister Liliana is riding on Ashley's lap.

Take Aways

1. **God Speaks Through Prayer, Worship and Praise.**
   Do not be anxious about anything, but in every situation, by prayer and petition, with thanksgiving, present your requests to God. And the peace of God, which transcends all understanding, will guard your hearts and your minds in Christ Jesus,   -Philippians 4:6-7

2. God speaks through His Holy Spirit.
   When the Spirit of truth comes, he will guide you into all the truth, for he will not speak on his own authority, but whatever he hears he will speak, and he will declare to you the things that are to come. -John 16:13 NLT

3. When we spend time praising and worshipping God, we will start to recognize His Voice.
   "Very truly I tell you Pharisees, anyone who does not enter the sheep pen by the gate, but climbs in by some other way, is a thief and a robber. The one who enters by the gate is the shepherd of the sheep. The gatekeeper opens the gate for him, and the sheep listen to his voice. He calls his own sheep by name and leads them out. When he has brought out all his own, he goes on ahead of them, and his sheep follow him because they know his voice. But they will never follow a stranger; in fact, they will run away from him because they do not recognize a stranger's voice." - John 10:1-5

4. God has given us armor to put on and wear every day.
   Finally, be strong in the Lord and in his mighty power. Put on the full armor of God, so that you can take your stand against the devil's schemes. For our struggle is not against flesh and blood, but against the rulers, against the authorities, against the powers of this dark world and against the spiritual forces of evil in the heavenly realms. Therefore, put on the full armor of God, so that when the day of evil comes, you may be able to stand your ground, and after you have done everything, to stand. Stand firm then, with the belt of truth buckled around your waist, with the breastplate of righteousness in place, and with your feet fitted with the readiness that comes from the gospel of peace. In addition to all this, take up the shield of faith, with which you can extinguish all the flaming

arrows of the evil one. Take the helmet of salvation and the sword of the Spirit, which is the word of God.
- Ephesians 6:10-18

5. God protects us from the evil of this world and the evil in the spirit world that is invisible to us.
But the Lord is faithful. He will establish you and guard you against the evil one. -Thessalonians 3:3 ESV

No weapon that is fashioned against you shall succeed, and you shall confute every tongue that rises against you in judgment. This is the heritage of the servants of the LORD and their vindication from me, declares the LORD.
- Isaiah 54:17 ESV

ACKNOWLEDGEMENTS

Thank you to my Lord and Savior Jesus Christ, God the Father and the sweet Holy Spirit without Whom none of this would have been possible.

Lord of my life, thank you for allowing me to join You in the journey of writing this book. It has been my honor and privilege to record the God Stories written within these pages...the stories You have written into our lives throughout the last five decades.

Lord, when we started this project, I had no idea where the road would lead or what the end would look like...but You knew God. Thank you for guiding me and giving me each word and each piece of the puzzle in the exact moment I needed them. Please bless all those who read these stories and please use them to change the lives of many.

ABOUT THE AUTHOR

Born and raised in Grand Rapids, Michigan, before moving to Sanford, Michigan, Renee Allen is an accomplished teacher, coach, writer and photographer. Renee has spent her life working with children of all ages. Over the past four decades she has documented the "God Stories" of her life in more than 20 handwritten journals. The stories in those journals are now the heartbeat of *Mommy, How Does God Speak to You?*

Renee has been involved in either Bible Study Fellowship (BSF) or Community Bible Study (CBS) for over 35 years. She is a trained and certified Teen CBS Assistant Director. A teacher and coach for over 40 years, Renee has always been known as an accomplished leader of her trade having spoken at numerous seminars and held various leadership positions in a number of professional organizations. In addition, Renee has spent the last more than 20 years writing, editing, publishing and photographing various West Midland Family Center (WMFC) publications.

Renee currently lives in Central Florida with her husband Mike, pursuing her lifelong dream of writing.

Made in the USA
Columbia, SC
23 April 2024

34548371R00104